Workbook to Accompany Kaplan and Saccuzzo's

Psychological Testing

Principles, Applications, and Issues

Second Edition

Carma Heitzmann
Veterans Administration Medical Center
Palo Alto

Brooks/Cole Publishing Company
Pacific Grove, California

Brooks/Cole Publishing Company
A Division of Wadsworth, Inc.

Printed in the United States of America

10 9 8 7 6 5 4 3 2 1

ISBN 0-534-09517-8

Sponsoring Editor: Phil Curson
Editorial Assistant: Heather L. Riedl
Production Coordinator: Dorothy Bell
Cover Design: Lisa Thompson

Preface

The *Workbook to Accompany Kaplan and Saccuzzo's Psychological Testing: Principles, Applications, and Issues* (2nd ed.) was designed to assist the student in understanding and applying the issues presented in the textbook. It should also be useful in assisting students to prepare for examinations. The workbook is meant to supplement the textbook material and each chapter should be completed following a careful reading of the corresponding text. Each workbook chapter is divided into a number of sections.

The first section in each chapter asks the reader to identify important terms, concepts, and names. It is recommended that the student attempt to complete this section before continuing through the workbook chapter, since it provides the foundation for the remainder of the exercises. These items are presented again at the end of the chapter along with the page numbers on which they can be located in the textbook.

Second, fill-in questions are presented. Answers and corresponding page numbers for further reference are found at the end of the chapter.

Third, a number of multiple-choice questions are provided. Again, the answers and corresponding textbook page numbers are listed in the answer section. These and the fill-in questions are intended not only to assist the student in understanding the issues involved in psychological testing, but also to illustrate the types of questions one might encounter on an examination.

Computational problems comprise the fourth feature of the workbook. These are found only in those chapters referring to statistical methods. In the answer section these problems have been worked out in an easy to follow, step-by-step fashion. Whether or not your instructor requires you to calculate similar problems on exams, these exercises will help to famililiarize you with some of the applied aspects of statistics in psychology.

Finally, thought questions are presented. In most cases these questions ask you to apply the information found in the textbook to a novel situation or to go somewhat beyond the material that is presented. When appropriate, the relevant textbook page numbers are provided. The primary purposes of this section are to stimulate thought and discussion and to challenge the student to think about psychological testing and measurement in a more global context.

Contents

Chapter 1

Introduction

Terms, Concepts, and Names

Briefly identify the following:

test____

psychological test______________________________

overt behavior________________________________

covert behavior_______________________________

individual test________________________________

group test___________________________________

achievement__________________________________

aptitude____________________________________

intelligence__________________________________

human ability_________________________________

personality test______________________________

structured personality test______________________________________

projective personality test______________________________________

psychological testing______________________________________

principles of psychological testing______________________________________

Charles Darwin______________________________________

Sir Frances Galton______________________________________

James McKeen Cattell______________________________________

Wilhelm Wundt______________________________________

Alfred Binet______________________________________

Binet-Simon Scale______________________________________

standardization sample______________________________________

representative sample______________________________________

Robert Yerkes______________________________________

Army Alpha

Army Beta

Wechsler-Bellvue Intelligence Scale

trait

Woodworth Personal Data Sheet

Rorschach

David Levy

Sam Beck

Henry Murray

Christina Morgan

Thematic Apperception Test (TAT)

Minnesota Multiphasic Personality Inventory (MMPI)

California Psychological Inventory (CPI)

factor analysis

Sixteen Personality Factor (16PF)______________________________
____
____

Shakow report_____________________________________
____
____

Fill-in Questions

1. A(n) __________ behavior is one that takes place within an individual and cannot be observed. On the other hand, __________ behaviors are observable.
2. A psychological test measuring present behavior attempts to determine ____________________.
3. __________ refers to the potential for learning a specific skill.
4. Two types of personality tests are ____________________ and ____________________.
5. The type of personality test that requires an individual to choose between two or more alternative responses is a(n) ________________ ____________________.
6. The western world most likely learned about testing programs through exposure to the __________.
7. The most basic concept underlying psychological testing is that of ____________________.
8. The first systematic attempt to evaluate individual differences in human intelligence was by __________.
9. A major difference between the Stanford-Binet and Wechsler-Bellvue Intelligence tests is that ____________________________________ ______________________________________.
10. One of the goals of traditional personality testing is to measure __________.
11. The test stimulus for structured personality tests tends to be __________, while projective tests provide a(n) __________ stimulus.
12. Factor analytic techniques were employed in the development of the __________.

13. During the 1940s and early 1950s ____________________ was the major function of clinical psychologists.

Multiple-Choice Questions

1. The use of test batteries was common by the time of the
   a) Ling Dynasty
   b) Han Dynasty
   c) Ming Dynasty
   d) Tam Dynasty
   e) Nam Dynasty

2. The term "mental test" was coined by
   a) James McKeen Cattell
   b) Charles Darwin
   c) Sir Frances Galton
   d) Alfred Binet
   e) Robert Yerkes

3. Who headed the team of psychologists that developed the Army Alpha and Army Beta?
   a) James McKeen Cattell
   b) Alfred Binet
   c) L. M. Terman
   d) Robert Yerkes
   e) J. F. Herbart

4. Which of the following is a group test of human ability for adults that does not require the subject to be literate?
   a) Army Alpha
   b) Seguin Form Board
   c) Stanford-Binet
   d) Army Beta
   e) Wechsler-Bellvue Intelligence Scale

5. The first structured personality test was the
   a) MMPI
   b) Rorschach
   c) Woodworth Personal Data Sheet

d) TAT
e) 16PF

6. The Rorschach was introduced into the United States by
   a) Sam Beck
   b) Herman Rorschach
   c) Christina Morgan
   d) Henry Murray
   e) David Levy

7. Which of the following personality tests is purported to measure human needs?
   a) Rorschach
   b) MMPI
   c) TAT
   d) CPI
   e) 16PF

Thought Questions

1. Explain the purpose of a standardization sample and discuss the characteristics such a sample should possess. How might you go about obtaining such a sample? (page12)

2. In what settings are psychological tests most likely to be found today? What role does psychological testing play in contemporary society and how has this role changed since the inception of testing? (pages 9-21)

Answers

Terms, Concepts, and Names

test (p.4)
psychological test (p.4)
overt behavior (p.4)
covert behavior (p.4)
individual test (p.5)
group test (p.5)
achievement (p.5)
aptitude (p.5)
intelligence (p.5)
human ability (p.6)
personality test (p.6)

structured personality test (p.6)
projective personality test (p.6)
psychological testing (p.6)
principles of psychological testing (p.7)
Charles Darwin (p.9)
Sir Frances Galton (p.10)
James McKeen Cattell (p.10)
Wilhelm Wundt (p.11)
Alfred Binet (p.12)
Binet-Simon Scale (p.12)
standardization sample (p.12)
representative sample (p.12)
Robert Yerkes (p.13)
Army Alpha (p.13)
Army Beta (p.13)
Wechsler-Bellvue Intelligence Scale (p.14)
trait (p.15)
Woodworth Personal Data Sheet (p.15)
Rorschach (p.16)
David Levy (p.16)
Sam Beck (p.16)
Henry Murray (p.16)
Christina Morgan (p.16)
TAT (p.16)
MMPI (p.17)
CPI (p.17)
factor analysis (p.17)
16PF (p.18)
Shakow report (p.18)

<u>Fill-in Questions</u>

1. covert, overt (p.4)
2. current functioning (p.4)
3. Aptitude (p.5)
4. structured personality tests, projective personality tests (p.6)
5. structured personality test (p.6)
6. Chinese (p.9)
7. individual differences (p.10)
8. Binet (p.12)

9. the Wechsler-Bellvue yields several scores/the Wechsler-Bellvue contains a performance scale (p.14)
10. traits (p.15)
11. unambiguous, ambiguous (p.16)
12. 16PF (p.18)
13. psychological testing (p.18)

Multiple-Choice Questions

1. b (p.9)
2. a (p.10)
3. d (p.13)
4. d (p.13)
5. c (p.15)
6. e (p.16)
7. c (p.17)

Chapter 2

Norms and Basic Statistics for Testing

Terms, Concepts and Names

Briefly identify the following:

descriptive statistics________________________________

exploratory data analysis________________________________

confirmatory data analysis________________________________

inferential statistics________________________________

sample________________________________

magnitude________________________________

equal intervals________________________________

absolute zero________________________________

nominal scale________________________________

ordinal scale________________________________

interval scale____

ratio scale

frequency distribution

frequency polygon

percentile rank

percentiles

variable

mean

variance

standard deviation

z score

standard normal distribution

McCall's T

quartile____

____

____

decile____

____

____

stanine____

____

____

norms____

____

____

tracking____

____

____

Fill-in Questions

1. The purpose of a __________ scale is to name objects.
2. __________ scales have the properties of magnitude and equal intervals, while __________ scales have the properties of magnitude, equal intervals, and absolute zero.
3. The variance of a set of scores is the mean of the _______________________________ and is calculated by _______________, _______________, and _______________.
4. The standard deviation is the _______________ of the variance and is represented by _____ when it refers to a population and _____ when it refers to a sample.
5. If a score is equal to the mean its z score will be _____. If the score is greater than the mean the z score will be __________ and if it is less than the mean the z score will be __________.
6. __________ scores are standard scores with a mean of 50 and a standard deviation of 10.

Multiple-Choice Questions

1. A scale which allows us to rank individuals or objects but not to say anything about the meaning of the differences between the ranks is a(n)
   a) nominal scale
   b) interval scale
   c) ordinal scale
   d) ratio scale
   e) magnitude scale

2. In a bell-shaped curve the greatest frequency of scores is near the
   a) ends of the distribution
   b) center of the distribution
   c) top of the distribution
   d) bottom of the distribution
   e) cannot say without knowing the range of scores

3. Approximately what percentage of scores fall below the mean in a standard normal distribution?
   a) 50%
   b) 34%
   c) 1%
   d) 84%
   e) 16%

4. At approximately what percentile would a score be that is two standard deviations below the mean in a standard normal distribution?
   a) 16th
   b) 5th
   c) 34th
   d) 2nd
   e) 50th

5. Within the quartile system the third quartile is what percentile?
   a) 50th
   b) 25th

c) 30th
d) 75th
e) 60th

6. What system is standardized to have a mean of 5 and a standard deviation of approximately 2?
a) decile
b) McCall's T
c) stanine
d) quartile
e) z score

Computational Problems

1. Determine what your percentile rank would be if you received the tenth highest grade on your psychology exam in a class of 50 students.

2. Find the mean for each of the following sets of numbers.
a)6,4,2,9

mean=__________

b)5,8,10,3

mean=__________

c)14,0,5,8,6

mean=__________

3. For each of the following sets of numbers calculate the standard deviation using both the deviation and raw score methods found on page 39 of your text. (Note: Use the formula for samples.)

a)8
5
3
4
7
5

deviation__________

raw score__________

b)12
15
20
8
5

deviation___________

raw score___________

c)5
10
12
30
0

deviation__________

raw score__________

4. Find the z score equivalents for the following scores using the formula on page 39 of your text.

a)10 z score______

b)5 z score______

c)3 z score______

d)6 z score______

5. Calculate the raw score equivalents of the following z scores given a mean of 10 and a standard deviation of 2.

a)-2.0

raw score__________

b).5

raw score__________

c)1.5

raw score__________

Thought Questions

1. What purposes do statistical methods serve in our quest for scientific understanding? (page 22)

____

____

____

____

____

____

2. What information do norms provide and what possible inadequacies might a given set of norms have?

____

____

____

3. What is the difference between a norm-referenced test and a criterion-referenced test? Give a unique example of each.

Answers

Terms, Concepts, and Names

descriptive statistics (p.23)
exploratory data analysis (p.23)
confirmatory data analysis (p.23)
inferential statistics (p.24)
sample (p.24)
magnitude (p.24)
equal intervals (p.25)
absolute zero (p.26)
nominal scale (p.26)
ordinal scale (p.26)
interval scale (p.27)
ratio scale (p.27)
frequency distribution (p.28)
frequency polygon (p.29)
percentile rank (p.30)
percentiles (p.33)
variable (p.34)

standard deviation (p.37)
z score (p.38)
standard normal distribution (p.39)
McCall's T (p.44)
quartile (p.45)
decile (p.45)
stanine (p.45)
norms (p.47)
tracking (p.48)

Fill-in Questions

1. nominal (p.26)
2. interval, ratio (p.27)
3. squared deviations around the mean, squaring each deviation, summing them, dividing by N (p.37)
4. square root, σ, S (pp.37-38)
5. 0, positive, negative (p.38)
6. McCall's T (p.44)

Multiple-Choice Questions

1. c (p.26)
2. b (p.28)
3. a (p.40)
4. d (p.41)
5. d (p.45)
6. c (p.45)

Computational Problems

1. 1. Determine how many people obtained a score below the score of interest. 50-10=40
2. Determine how many people were in the group. 50
3. Divide the number of people below the score of interest (Step1) by

2. Determine how many people were in the group. 50
3. Divide the number of people below the score of interest (Step1) by the number of people in the group (Step 2). 40÷50=.80
4. Multiply the result of this division (Step 3) by 100. .80x100=80
5. Percentile rank=**80th**

2. a)6+4+2+9=21
21÷4=5.25
x=**5.25**
b)5+8+10+3=26
26÷4=6.5
x=**6.5**
c)14+0+5+8+6=33
33÷5=6.6
x=**6.6**

3. a)

Deviation Method:

1. Find N by counting the number of observations.
N=6
2. Find N-1. Subtract 1 from Step 1.
6-1=5
3. Find $\overline{X}$. Add up all of the scores and divide by the number of scores (Step 1).
8+5..........+5=32
32÷6=5.33
4. Find X-$\overline{X}$. Subtract $\overline{X}$ (Step 3) from each score.
8-5.33=2.67
5-5.33=-.33
3-5.33=-2.33
4-5.33=-1.33
7-5.33=1.67
5-5.33=-.33
5. Find $\Sigma(X-\overline{X})^2$. Square each of the results from Step 4 and add them up.
$(2.67^2)+(-.33^2)+(-2.33^2)+(-1.33^2)+(1.67^2)+(-.33^2)=$
7.13+.11..........+.11=17.33
6. Find $S=\sqrt{\frac{\Sigma(X-\overline{X})^2}{N-1}}$. Divide Step 5 by Step 2 and take the square root.

$$\sqrt{\frac{17.33}{5}} = \sqrt{3.47} = 1.86$$

S=1.86

<u>Raw Score Method</u>:

1. Find N by counting the number of observations.

   N=6

2. Find N-1. Subtract 1 from Step 1.

   6-1=5

3. Find ΣX^2. Square each score and then add them up.

   $8^2+5^2 .... +5^2=$

   64+25..........+25=188

4. Find $(\Sigma X)^2$. Add up all of the scores and square the result.

   8+5..........+5=32

   32^2=1,024

5. Find $\frac{(\Sigma X)^2}{N}$. Divide Step 4 by Step 1.

   1,024÷6=170.67

6. Find $\Sigma X^2 - \frac{(\Sigma X)^2}{N}$. Subtract the result of Step 5 from the result of Step 3.

   188-170.67=17.33

7. Find $S = \sqrt{\frac{\Sigma X^2 - \frac{(\Sigma X)^2}{N}}{N-1}}$. Divide the result of Step 6 by the result of Step 2 and take the square root.

   $$\sqrt{\frac{17.33}{5}} = \sqrt{3.47} = 1.86$$

   S=1.86

b)

<u>Deviation Method:</u>

1. Find N by counting the number of observations.

   N=5

2. Find N-1. Subtract 1 from Step 1.

   5-1=4

3. Find $\overline{X}$. Add up all of the scores and divide by the number (N) of scores (Step 1).

   12+15..........+5=60

   60÷5=12

4. Find $X-\bar{X}$. Subtract $\bar{X}$ (Step 3) from each score.

   12-12=0

   15-12=3

   20-12=8

   8-12=-4

   5-12=-7

5. Find $\Sigma(X-\bar{X})^2$. Square each of the results from Step 4 and add them up.

   $(0^2)+(3^2)+(8^2)+(-4^2)+(-7^2)=$

   0+9+64+16+49=138

6. Find $S=\sqrt{\frac{\Sigma(X-\bar{X})^2}{N-1}}$. Divide Step 5 by Step 2 and take the square root.

   $\sqrt{\frac{138}{4}}=\sqrt{34.5}=5.87$

   S=5.87

Raw Score Method:

1. Find N. Count the number of observations.

   N=5

2. Find N-1. Subtract 1 from Step 1.

   5-1=4

3. Find ΣX^2. Square each score and then add them up.

   $12^2+15^2+20^2+8^2+5^2=$

   144+225=..........+25=858

4. Find $(\Sigma X)^2$. Add up all of the scores and square the result.

   12+15..........+5=60

   $60^2=3{,}600$

5. Find $\frac{(\Sigma X)^2}{N}$. Divide Step 4 by Step 1.

   3,600÷5=720

6. Find $\Sigma X^2-\frac{(\Sigma X)^2}{N}$. Subtract the result of Step 5 from the result of Step 3.

   858-720=138

7. Find $S=\sqrt{\frac{\Sigma X^2-\frac{(\Sigma X)^2}{N}}{}}$. Divide the result of Step 6 by the result of Step 2 and take the square root.

   $\sqrt{\frac{138}{4}}=\sqrt{34.5}=5.87$

   S=5.87

c)

Deviation Method:

1. Find N. Count the number of observations.

   N=5

2. Find N-1. Subtract 1 from Step 1.

   5-1=4

3. Find $\overline{X}$. Add up all of the scores and divide by the number (N) of scores (Step 1).

   5+10..........+0=57

   57÷5=11.4

4. Find X-$\overline{X}$. Subtract $\overline{X}$ (Step 3) from each score.

   5-11.4=-6.4

   10-11.4=-1.4

   12-11.4=.6

   30-11.4=18.6

   0-11.4=-11.4

5. Find $\Sigma(X-\overline{X})^2$. Square each of the results from Step 4 and add them up.

   $(-6.4^2)+(-1.4^2)..........+(0^2)=$

   40.96+1.96..........+129.96=519.2

6. Find $S=\sqrt{\frac{\Sigma(X-\overline{X})^2}{N-1}}$. Divide Step 5 by Step 2 and take the square root.

   $\sqrt{\frac{519.20}{4}} = \sqrt{129.8} = 11.39$

   S=11.39

Raw Score Method:

1. Find N. Count the number of observations.

   N=5

2. Find N-1. Subtract 1 from Step 1.

   5-1=4

3. Find ΣX^2. Square each score and then add them.

   $5^2+10^2..........+0^2=$

   25+100..........+0=1,169

4. Find $(\Sigma X)^2$. Add up all of the scores and square the result.

   5+10.........+0=57

   $57^2=3{,}249$

5. Find $\frac{(\sum X)^2}{N}$. Divide Step 4 by Step 1.

$3{,}249 \div 5 = 649.8$

6. Find $\sum X^2 - \frac{(\sum X)^2}{N}$. Subtract the result of Step from the result of Step 3.

$1{,}169 - 649.8 = 519.2$

7. Find $S = \sqrt{\frac{\sum X^2 - \frac{(\sum X)^2}{N}}{N-1}}$. Divide the result of Step 6 by the result of Step 2 and take the square root.

$\sqrt{\frac{519.2}{4}} = \sqrt{129.8} = 11.39$

S=11.39

4.

1. Find N. Count the number of observations.

N=4

2. Find N-1. Subtract 1 from Step 1.

4-1=3

3. Find $\overline{X}$. Add up all of the scores and divide by the number (N) of scores (Step1).

10+5+3+6=24

$24 \div 4 = 6$

4. Find $X-\overline{X}$. Subtract $\overline{X}$ (Step 3) from each score.

10-6=4

5-6=4

3-6=3

6-6=0

5. Find $\sum(X-\overline{X})^2$. Square each of the results from Step 4 and add them up.

$(4^2)+(-1^2)+(-3^2)+(0^2)=$

16+1+9+0=26

6. Find $S = \sqrt{\frac{\sum(X-\overline{X})^2}{N-1}}$. Divide Step 5 by Step 2 and take the square root.

$\sqrt{\frac{26}{3}} = \sqrt{8.67} = 2.94$

7. Find the z score equivalents using the formula: $z = \frac{X - \overline{X}}{S}$;

a) $z = \frac{10-6}{2.94} = \frac{4}{2.94} =$ **1.36**

b) $z = \frac{5-6}{2.94} = \frac{-1}{2.94} =$ **-.34**

c) $z = \frac{3-6}{2.94} = \frac{-3}{2.94} =$ **-1.02**

d) $z = \frac{6-6}{2.94} = \frac{0}{2.94} =$ **0**

5.

Using the formula: $z = \frac{X - \overline{X}}{S}$;

a) $-2.0 = \frac{X-10}{2} = 10+(2.0)(-2)=X$ **X=6**

b) $.5 = \frac{X-10}{2} = 10+(.5)(2)=X$ **X=11**

c) $1.5 = \frac{X-10}{2} = 10+(1.5)(2)=X$ **X=13**

Chapter 3

Correlation and Regression

Terms, Concepts, and Names

Briefly identify the following:

scatter diagram____
____
____

correlation____
____
____

regression line____
____
____

Pearson Product Moment Correlation Coefficient__________________
____
____

normative____
____
____

Spearman's rho____
____
____

biserial correlation____
____
____

phi coefficient____
____
____

residual____
____
____

standard error of estimate_____________________________________
____

coefficient of determination____
____
____

coefficient of alienation____
____
____

shrinkage____
____
____

cross-validation____
____
____

multivariate methods____
____
____

discriminant analysis____
____
____

factor analysis____
____
____

principal components____
____
____

factor loadings____
____
____

Fill-in Questions

1. Each point on a scatter diagram represents ________________________
________________.

2. If the line that comes closest to all the points in a scatter diagram is straight, the correlation between the two variables is __________; however, if the line is curved the correlation is __________.
3. If the scores on X do not give us any information about the scores on Y this indicates ______________________.
4. The regression line is the best-fitting straight line through a set of points in a scatter diagram. It is found by using the principle of ______________.
5. The __________ describes how much change is expected in Y each time X increases by one unit.
6. In a correlation the scores for both variables are in __________ units and the intercept is always __________.
7. The Pearson Product Moment Correlation Coefficient can take any value between __________ and __________.
8. Correlation coefficients can be tested for statistical significance using the __________.
9. The ____________________ is a measure of accuracy of prediction in a correlation and is the standard deviation of the ______________.
10. Correlational techniques only allow us to describe the relationship between two variables, whereas ____________________ allow us to examine the relationships among many variables.

Multiple-Choice Questions

1. In the two scatter diagrams shown below the relationship between the two variables is
   a) stronger in A than in B
   b) equal in A and B
   c) impossible to determine
   d) stronger in B than in A
   e) none of the above

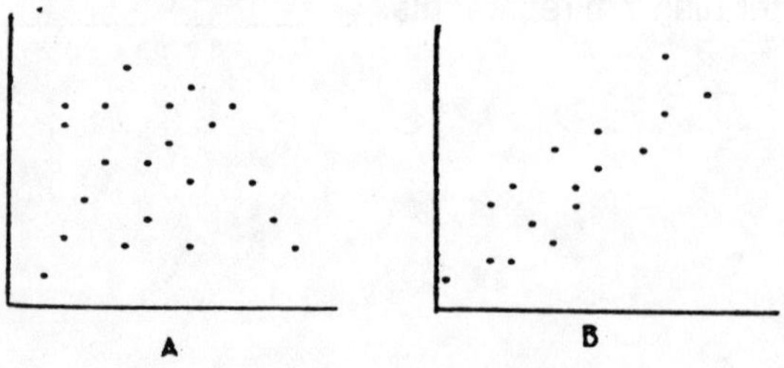

2. People who drink caffeinated beverages tend to experience increased alertness and psychomotor activity. This demonstrates a
   a) positive correlation
   b) negative correlation
   c) zero correlation
   d) not enough information is provided
   e) none of the above

3. Which of the following correlations represents the strongest relationship between two variables?
   a) .50
   b) .00
   c) -.85
   d) .80
   e) -.10

4. In the formula Y'=a+bx, Y' is the
   a) regression coefficient
   b) raw score of Y
   c) predicted value of Y
   d) intercept
   e) slope

5. The point at which the regression line crosses the Y axis is the
   a) slope
   b) regression coefficient
   c) predicted value of X
   d) correlation
   e) intercept

6. A method of correlation that is used to find the association between two sets of ranks rather than between continuous variables is

a) Spearman's rho
b) point biserial
c) tetrachoric
d) phi coefficient
e) Pearson Product Moment

7. In order to determine the relationship between sex of subject and income level one would use the
   a) phi coefficient
   b) point biserial correlation
   c) Spearman's rho
   d) Pearson Product Moment Correlation Coefficient
   e) any of the above would be suitable

8. The primary purpose of factor analysis is to
   a) determine the relationship between variables
   b) reduce a large set of variables to a smaller composite set
   c) predict some criterion
   d) insure that proper inferences are being made
   e) determine the degree of non-association between variables

Computational Problems

1. An epidemiologist is interested in determining the effect of immunization against chicken pox on the rate of the disease in children. To do so, she sampled six cities across the country and established both the percentage of children who had been vaccinated and the number of cases of chicken pox per 100 children. Find the correlation coefficient for these two variables using the formula found on page 62 of your text.

	X % of children immunized against chicken pox	Y # of cases of chicken pox per 100 children
A	43	6
B	72	4
C	81	3
D	32	7
E	19	13
F	84	2

2.a) Find the correlation coefficient for the following set of scores.

	X body weight	Y number of calories consumed per day (in hundreds)
A	150	20
B	110	18
C	200	30
D	105	12
E	175	21

b) Explain in words the meaning of the resulting correlation coefficient.

c) Plot this relationship on the figure below.

d) What percentage of total variation in the scores on Y can be explained by our information about X?

e) Find the coefficient of alienation.

<u>Thought Questions</u>

1. Select a variable of interest and a hypothetical means of predicting it, and plot the relationship on the figure below. In words, explain your diagram.

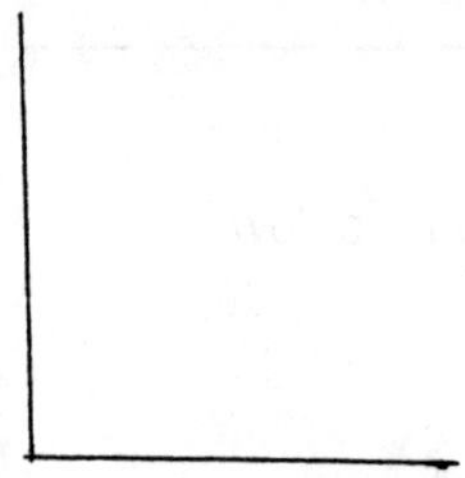

2. Explain the correlation-causation problem and give an example. (page 77)

3. Discuss possible third variables that may explain the observed relationship between the variables in the second computational problem.

Answers

Terms, Concepts, and Names

scatter diagram (p.55)
correlation (p.57)
regression line (p.59)
Pearson Product Moment Correlation Coefficient (p.63)
normative (p.69)
Spearman's rho (p.73)
biserial correlation (p.74)
phi coefficient (p.74)
residual (p.75)
standard error of estimate (p.76)
coefficient of determination (p.76)

coefficient of alienation (p.76)
shrinkage (p.76)
cross-validation (p.77)
multivariate methods (p.78)
discriminant analysis (p.80)
factor analysis (p.81)
principal components (p.82)
factor loadings (p.82)

Fill-in Questions

1. where an individual scored on both X and Y (p.56)
2. linear, non-linear (pp.56-57)
3. no correlation (p.57)
4. least squares (p. 59)
5. slope (p.60)
6. z or standard, zero (p.63)
7. -1.0, 1.0 (p.63)
8. t-distribution (p.68)
9. standard error of estimate, residuals (p.75-76)
10. multivariate methods (p.78)

Multiple-Choice Questions

1. d
2. a
3. c
4. c (p.59)
5. e (p.60)
6. a (p.73)
7. b (p.74)
8. b (p.81)

Computational Problems

1.

1. Find N by counting the number of paired observations.
   N=6
2. Find $\sum X$ by summing the X scores.
   43+72..........+84=331

3. Find ΣY by summing the Y scores.

6+4.........+2=35

4. Find ΣX^2. Square each X score and then add them up.

1849+5184..........+7,056=22,035

5. Find ΣY^2. Square each Y score and then add them up.

36+16..........+4=283

6. Find ΣXY. For each pair of observations multiply X by Y and then add up the products.

(43x6)+(72x4)..........+(84x2)=

258+288..........+168=1,428

7. Find $(\Sigma X)^2$ by squaring the result of Step 2.

331^2=109,561

8. Find $(\Sigma Y)^2$ by squaring the result of Step 3.

35^2=1,225

9. Find $N\Sigma XY$ by multiplying the results of Steps 1 and 6.

6x1,428=8,568

10. Find $(\Sigma X)(\Sigma Y)$ by multiplying the results of Steps 2 and 3.

331x35=11,585

11. Find $N\Sigma XY-(\Sigma X)(\Sigma Y)$ by subtracting the results of Step 10 from the results of Step 9.

8,568-11,585=-3,017

12. Find $N\Sigma X^2$ by multiplying the results of Steps 1 and 4.

6x22,035=132,210

13. Find $N\Sigma X^2-(\Sigma X)^2$ by subtracting the results of Step 7 from Step 12.

132,210-109,561=22,649

14. Find $N\Sigma Y^2$ by multiplying the results of Steps 1 and 5.

6x283=1,698

15. Find $N\Sigma Y^2$ by subtracting the results of Step 8 from Step 14.

1,698-1,225=473

16. Find $\sqrt{[N\Sigma X^2-(\Sigma X)^2][N\Sigma Y^2-(\Sigma Y)^2]}$ by multiplying the results of Steps 13 and 15 and then taking the square root of the product.

$\sqrt{22,649x473}$ = $\sqrt{10,712,977}$ =3,273.07

17. Find $r = \dfrac{N\Sigma XY-(\Sigma X)(\Sigma Y)}{\sqrt{[N\Sigma X^2-(\Sigma X)^2][N\Sigma Y^2-(\Sigma Y)^2]}}$.

by dividing the results of Step 11 by Step 16.

-3,017÷3,273.07=-.92

r=-.92

2. a)

1. Find N by counting the number of paired observations.
   N=5
2. Find ΣX by summing the X scores.
   150+110+200+105+175=740
3. Find ΣY by summing the Y scores.
   20+18+30+12+21=101
4. Find ΣX^2. Square each X score and then add them up.
   22,500+12,100+40000+11,025+30,625=116,250
5. Find ΣY^2. Square each Y score and then add them up.
   400+324+900+144+441=2,209
6. Find ΣXY. For each pair of observations multiply X by Y. Then add up the products.
   (150x20)+(110x18)......=
   3,000+1,980+6,000+1,260+3,675=15,915
7. Find $(\Sigma X)^2$ by squaring the result of Step 2.
   740^2=547,600
8. Find $(\Sigma Y)^2$ by squaring the result of Step 3.
   101^2=10,201
9. Find $N\Sigma XY$ by multiplying the results of Steps 1 and 6.
   5x15,915=79,575
10. Find $(\Sigma X)(\Sigma Y)$ by multiplying the results of Steps 2 and 3.
   740x101=74,740
11. Find $N\Sigma XY-(\Sigma X)(\Sigma Y)$ by subtracting the results of Step 10 from the results of Step 9.
   79,575-74,740=4,835
12. Find $N\Sigma X^2$ by multiplying the results of Steps 1 and 4.
   5x116,250=581,250
13. Find $N\Sigma X^2-(\Sigma X)^2$ by subtracting the results of Step 7 from Step 12.
   58,1250-547,600=33,650
14. Find $N\Sigma Y^2$ by multiplying the results of Steps1and 5.
   5x2,209=11,045
15. Find $N\Sigma Y^2-(\Sigma Y)^2$ by subtracting the results of Step 8 from Step 14.
   11,045-10,201=844

16. Find $\sqrt{[N\Sigma X^2-(\Sigma X)^2][N\Sigma Y^2-(\Sigma Y)^2}$ by multiplying Steps 13 and 15 and then taking the square root of the product.

$\sqrt{33,650 \times 844} = \sqrt{28,400,600} = 5,329.22$

17. Find $r = \dfrac{N\Sigma XY-(\Sigma X)(\Sigma Y)}{\sqrt{[N\Sigma X^2-(\Sigma X)^2][N\Sigma Y^2-(\Sigma Y)^2}}$.

by dividing the results of Step11 by Step16.

$4,835 \div 5,329.22 = .91$

r=.91

b) A positive correlation coefficient of .91 indicates that there is a strong relationship between number of calories consumed per day and body weight. The more calories consumed the greater the weight.

c)

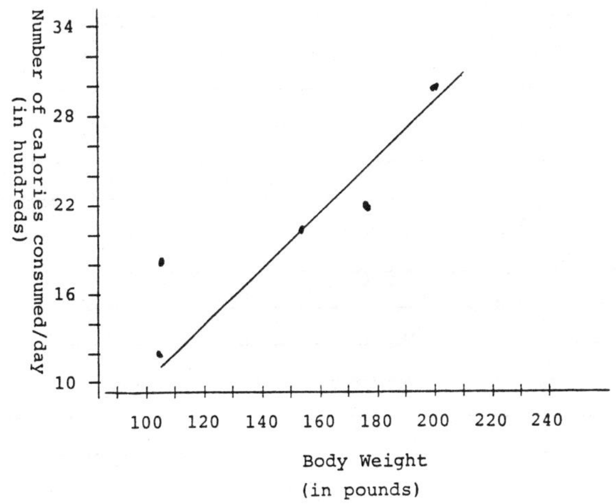

d) coefficient of determination= correlation coefficient squared or $.91^2$=**.83**

e) coefficient of alienation= the square root of 1-coefficient of determination or $\sqrt{1-.83} = \sqrt{.17}$=**.41**

Chapter 4

Reliability

Terms, Concepts, and Names

Briefly identify the following:

error in testing____________________

classical test score theory____________________

standard error of measurement____________________

test-retest reliability____________________

carry-over effect____________________

practice effect____________________

parallel forms____________________

domain sampling____________________

split-half method____________________

Spearman-Brown formula____________________

internal consistency____________________

Kuder-Richardson technique____

____

____

covariance____

____

____

Cronbach's alpha____

____

____

difference score____

____

____

prophecy formula____

____

____

discriminability analysis____

____

____

Fill-in Questions

1. Theoretically, an observed score is composed of __________ and __________.
2. Because classical test theory assumes that errors of measurement are random the distribution of errors should be __________.
3. The reliability coefficient is the ratio of the variance of the __________ of a test to the __________.
4. When the same group of people is administered the same test at two different points in time an assessment of _______________ is being made.
5. The Spearman-Brown formula corrects for ____________________.
6. All _______________ methods evaluate the extent to which different test items measure the same ability or trait.
7. Two approaches to improve the reliability of a test are to ____________________ and ________________________.
8. Attenuations of potential correlations are caused by _______________.

Multiple-Choice Questions

1. If a researcher is attempting to assess the reliability of a measure of depression the method of choice would be
   a) internal consistency
   b) time sampling
   c) the test-retest method
   d) both c and d
   e) both a and c

2. The odd-even system is an example of
   a) the split-half method
   b) internal consistency
   c) time sampling
   d) both a and b
   e) all of the above

3. The most conservative estimate of a test's split-half reliability is provided by
   a) the Spearman-Brown formula
   b) the Kuder-Richardson formula
   c) Cronbach's alphas
   d) the odd-even method
   e) the parallel forms method

4. Approximately what value must a reliability coefficient have for most purposes in basic research?
   a) .90
   b) .50
   c) .70
   d) .30
   e) 1.0

5. Under the rubric of the factor analytic approach to test construction, tests will be more reliable if they are
   a) lengthy
   b) multi-dimensional
   c) valid
   d) uni-dimensional
   e) criterion-referenced

Thought Questions

1. Discuss some of the problems facing an investigator who uses a measure with questionable reliability to assess a group of parents before and after a parent effectiveness workshop. (page 104)

2. Describe some of the advantages and disadvantages associated with behavioral observation techniques and provide an example. (page 106)

Answers

Terms, Names, and Concepts

error in testing (p.87)
classical test score theory (p.88)
standard error of measurement (p.90)
test-retest reliability (p.92)
carry-over effect (p.93)
practice effect (p.93)
parallel forms (p.94)
domain sampling (p.95)
split-half method (p.97)
Spearman-Brown formula (p.97)
internal consistency (p.99)
Kuder-Richardson technique (p.99)
covariance (p.100)
Cronbach's alpha (p.102)
difference score (p.104)
prophecy formula (p.112)
discriminability analysis (p.113)

Fill-in Questions

1. true score, error (p.89)
2. bell-shaped (p.89)
3. true score, observed score (p.91)
4. test-retest reliability (p.92)
5. deflated reliability due to half-length tests (p.97)
6. internal consistency (p.103)
7. increase the number of items, throw out items that decrease reliability (p.111)
8. measurement error (p.114)

Multiple-Choice Questions

1. a (pp.92 and 99)
2. d (pp.97 and 99)
3. b (p.101)
4. c (p.110)
5. d (p.113)

Chapter 5

Validity

Terms, Concepts, and Names

Briefly identify the following:

validity____

____

____

face validity____

____

____

content related validity____

____

____

criterion related validity____

____

____

predictive validity____

____

____

concurrent validity____

____

____

validity coefficient____

____

____

restricted range____

____

____

generalizability____

____

____

construct related validity____

____

____

convergent evidence____

____

____

discriminant evidence____
____
____

Fill-in Questions

1. Although not technically a form of validity _______________ implies that the items on a test are reasonably related to the perceived purpose of the test.
2. Two types of criterion related validity are __________ and __________.
3. __________ validity refers to the simultaneous relationship between the test and the criterion.
4. The correlation between a test and the criterion is referred to as a(n) ____________________.
5. The process of construct validation is necessary when no __________ is available which defines the object of inquiry.
6. To develop a test with construct validity both __________ and __________ evidence are essential.
7. Several measures are already available which are purported to assess anxiety. In order to prove that a new measure of anxiety is needed, the test must measure a __________ aspect of anxiety and, therefore, ____________________ of validity should be provided.

Multiple-Choice Questions

1. The evidence is logical rather than statistical for
   a) face validity and criterion related validity
   b) face validity and predictive validity
   c) criterion related validity and content related validity
   d) content related validity and face validity
   e) content related validity and concurrent validity

2. A test which allows us to identify individuals who are likely to become schizophrenic has
   a) face validity
   b) predictive validity
   c) criterion related validity
   d) both a and c
   e) both b and c

3. If, for example, a validity coefficient of .50 between a written test of driving ability and actual skills as a driver was found, what percentage of the variation in driving ability would be accounted for as a result of the information from the test?
   a) 10%
   b) 25%
   c) 5%
   d) 50%
   e) 1%

4. A variable with a "restricted range" is problematic with regard to the estimation of a validity coefficient due to a lack of
   a) criterion related validity
   b) variability
   c) adequate sample size
   d) cross validation
   e) representativeness

5. A researcher seeking to develop a measure of depression cites a moderate correlation between his or her measure and the Beck Depression Inventory as evidence of the test's validity. What type of validity documentation does this provide?
   a) convergent validity
   b) predictive validity
   c) discriminant validity
   d) content related validity
   e) face validity

Thought Questions

1. Choose a topic of interest and outline the types of items you would want to include in an assessment device to ensure that your measure has content related validity. Also discuss other factors that may influence an individual's performance on this test. (pages 119-120)

___

___

___

2. Select three of the seven recommended criteria for evaluation of validity coefficients found on pages 125-128 of your text, and develop a unique example of each that would demonstrate that a test may not be valid.

Answers

Terms, Concepts, and Names

validity (p.117)
face validity (p.119)
content related validity (p.119)
criterion related validity (p.121)
predictive validity (p.121)
concurrent validity (p.121)
validity coefficient (p.123)
restricted range (p.128)
generalizability (p.128)
construct related validity (p.131)
convergent evidence (p.133)
discriminant evidence (p.135)

Fill-in Questions

1. face validity (p.119)
2. predictive, concurrent (p.121)
3. concurrent (p.121)
4. validity coefficient (p.123)

5. criterion (p.131)
6. discriminant, convergent (p.133)
7. unique, discriminant evidence (p.135)

Multiple-Choice Questions

1. d (p.119)
2. e (p.121)
3. b (p.124)
4. b (p.128)
5. a (p.133)

Chapter 6

Building a Test

Terms, Concepts, and Names

Briefly identify the following:

dichotomous format

polychotomous format

distractors

Likert format

category format

Q-sort

item analysis

discrimination index

item characteristic curve

item response theory

internal criteria

criterion-referenced test

Fill-in Questions

1. Item reliability on multiple-choice tests is increased when the __________ chosen are likely to be selected as alternative responses.
2. Correction formulas are sometimes employed with tests having a polychotomous format in order to __________________________.
3. One difficulty that has been encountered with the use of __________ formats is that responses tend to be affected by the groupings of the items being rated.
4. The basic methods involved in item analysis are assessment of ___________________ and ____________________.
5. An optimum item difficulty level is usually about halfway between ____ and ____.
6. The __________ is the least frequent score in a frequency polygon and is used as a cutting point when evaluating the items in a criterion-referenced test.

Multiple-Choice Questions

1. A test format which is typically used for attitude measurement is the
   a) checklist format
   b) dichotomous format
   c) category format
   d) Likert format
   e) polychotomous format

2. One method for measuring chronic pain asks the respondent to group statements according to how accurately they describe his or her discomfort. This would be an example of the
   a) Q-sort format
   b) checklist format
   c) Likert format
   d) category format
   e) none of the above

3. If 50% of the individuals taking a particular test get a certain item correct the difficulty (or easiness) level of that item would be
   a) .05
   b) .25
   c) .50
   d) .10
   e) 2.5

4. The optimum difficulty level for a five choice multiple-choice item is approximately
   a) .625
   b) .600
   c) .500
   d) .665
   e) .584

5. The extreme group method is one way to determine
   a) item characteristic curves
   b) item discriminability
   c) item difficulty
   d) item reliability
   e) all of the above

6. Which of the following item characteristic curves displays the "best" test item?

a)

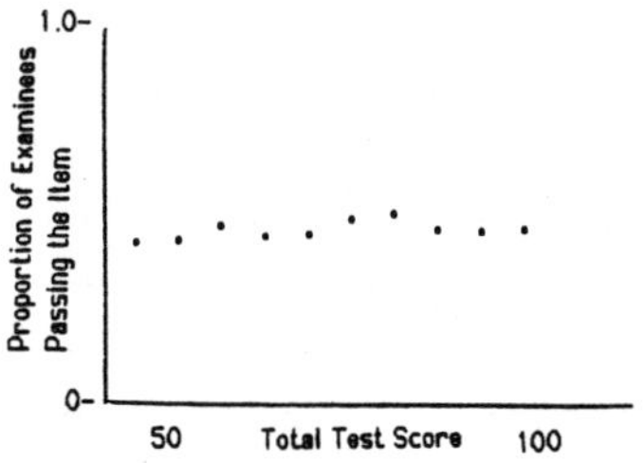

b)

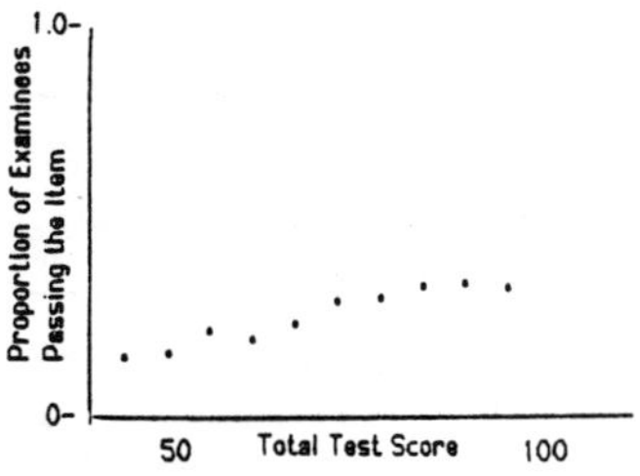

c)

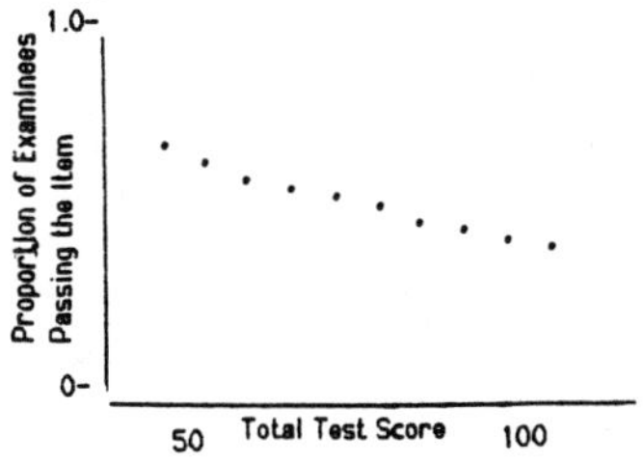

d)

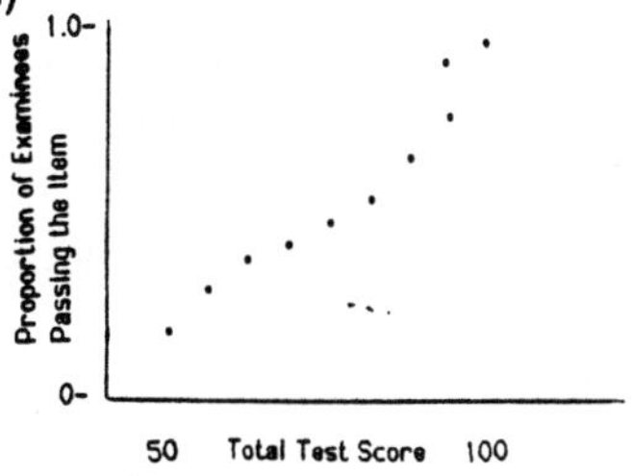

e)

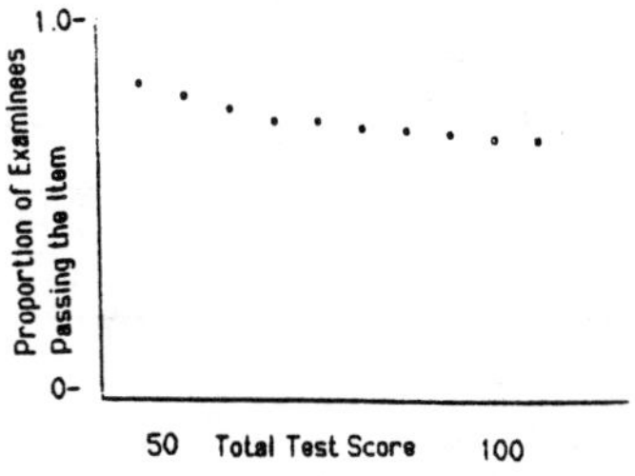

Thought Questions

1. Choose one of the item formats discussed on pages 140-146 of your text and describe a test that you might construct using this framework. Also provide your reasons for selecting this format and discuss some of its advantages and disadvantages.

2. Develop several test items and describe methods for analyzing the appropriateness or inappropriateness of their inclusion on a test. (Hint: It may be helpful to actually "administer" these items to a group of friends.)(pages 147-158)

Answers

Terms, Concepts, and Names

dichotomous format (p.140)
polychotomous format (p.141)
distractors (p.141)
Likert format (p.143)
category format (p.143)
Q-sort (p.144)
item analysis (p.147)
discrimination index (pp.149-150)
item characteristic curve (p.151)
item response theory (p.155)
internal criteria (p.156)
criterion-referenced test (p.157)

Fill-in Questions

1. distractors (p.141)
2. correct for guessing (p.142)
3. category (p.143)
4. item difficulty, item discriminability (p.147)
5. 100% of the respondents getting the item correct, level of success by chance alone (p.147)
6. antimode (p.157)

Multiple-Choice Questions

1. d (p.143)
2. a (p.144)
3. c (p.147)
4. b (p.147)
5. b (p.149)
6. d (pp.151-157)

Chapter 7

Selection and Personnel Decisions

Terms, Concepts, and Names

Briefly identify the following:

cutting score____

base rate____

hit rate____

false negatives____

false positives____

Taylor-Russell tables____

utility theory____

incremental validity____

Mental Measurement Yearbook____

Fill-in Questions

1. The ______________________ is a short booklet which provides a set of standards for test developers and users.
2. Among the questions that should be answered in a test manual are those

pertaining to practical considerations, scoring, __________, __________, and __________.

3. The hit rate of a test is ______________________________________.
4. In order for a test to be considered useful, it must provide more information than would be known from the __________ alone.
5. In terms of the Taylor-Russell tables, a test is most useful when the ______________ is high and the ______________ is low.
6. Success as defined by the Taylor-Russell tables requires that the criterion be a(n) __________ variable, whereas tables based on ______________ have attempted to define levels of success.
7. Tests should not be used unless they provide a significant __________ in information over what would be obtained with simpler methods.

Multiple-Choice Questions

1. On the basis of a psychological test an individual is identified as schizophrenic. An interview reveals schizophrenic thinking and a past history of psychiatric hospitalization. This case best illustrates a:
   a) false negative
   b) "miss"
   c) false positive
   d) "hit"
   e) both c and d

2. If a test were available that could identify those persons most likely to suffer heart attacks it would be **more costly and dangerous** to have a:
   a) high cutting score
   b) low cutting score
   c) false negative
   d) false positive
   e) both a and c

3. Health care professionals are often interested in being able to predict which patients are most likely to comply with medical recommendations. For example, it may be helpful to know in advance whether or not a hypertensive patient enrolled in a behavioral program to help him or her control his or her disease is likely to be successful, that is, to comply with program instructions. Let us assume that without any screening procedure 60% of such individuals are able to reduce their blood pressure following instruction. Unfortunately, only 50% of those persons interested in taking part in the program can be admitted. A newly developed paper and pencil measure designed to

evaluate the likelihood of medical compliance correlates .40 with actual patient adherence (i.e., success). Use the table on page 163 of your text to determine the usefulness of this test. On the basis of this measure the proportion of patients you would expect to be successful would be:

a) 79%
b) 73%
c) 70%
d) 83%
e) 80%

4. A program similar to the one described above can only select 40 out of 100 patients. Using the same base rate for success and validity coefficient, approximately how many of the persons you select can be expected to fail?
   a) 30
   b) 28
   c) 12
   d) 10
   e) 4

Thought Questions

1. Select a variable of interest that can be evaluated with some sort of test (i.e., medical, psychological, educational, etc.) and discuss the issues involved in determining an acceptable hit and miss rate. What would the base rate and cutting score be? What are the costs associated with false negatives and false positives? (pages 164-168)

2. Choose one of the reference books presented on pages 174-176 and describe a test which it reviews. Try to evaluate your selection based on the principles discussed thus far in your text.

Answers

Terms, Concepts, and Names:

cutting score (p.164)
base rate (p.165)
hit rate (p.165)
false negatives (p.166)
false positives (p.166)
Taylor-Russell tables (p.168)
utility theory (p.172)
incremental validity (p.173)
Mental Measurement Yearbook (p.175)

Fill-in Questions:

1. Standards for Educational and Psychological Tests (p. 163)
2. reliability, validity, standardization sample (pp.163-164)
3. the proportion of cases in which a test accurately predicts success or failure (p.165)
4. base rates (p.165)
5. validity of the test, selection ratio (p.170)
6. dichotomous, utility theory (p.172)
7. increment (p.173)

Multiple-Choice Questions:

1. d (p.165)
2. e (p.164-166)
3. b (pp.169)
4. d (pp.170-171) 75% of 40= 30
   40-30=10

Chapter 8

Test Administration

Terms, Concepts, and Names

Briefly identify the following:

expectancy effects____

____

____

Rosenthal effect____

____

____

reactivity____

____

____

drift____

____

____

partial correlation____

____

____

Fill-in Questions

1. Rosenthal asserted that expectancy effects are likely to result from subtle uses of ____________________ between the experimenter and the subject.
2. It is important to give tests under _____________________ because situational variables can affect test scores.
3. Students with _____________________ often have difficulty focusing on test items and may be distracted by intrusive thoughts. This is an example of a _____________________.
4. An increase in reliability referred to as ___________ is a reaction to being checked.

Multiple-Choice Questions

1. In general, studies have indicated that the race of the examiner
   a) should be the same as that of the subject
   b) should be different than that of the subject
   c) is not as important as sex of the examiner
   d) is only of importance with regard to intelligence tests
   e) is unrelated to test performance

2. Because reinforcement and feedback may damage the reliability and validity of test scores, most test manuals insist that
   a) feedback be given only by trained examiners
   b) no feedback be given
   c) feedback be given in a standardized manner
   d) feedback be given only if the subject appears to need encouragement
   e) feedback be given on a random basis

3. Which of the following is **not** an advantage of computer assisted test administration?
   a) performance dependent feedback
   b) patience
   c) control of bias
   d) excellence of standardization
   e) precision of timing responses

4. "Drift" refers to a problem inherent in the training of
   a) personality assessors
   b) intelligence testers
   c) test proctors
   d) behavioral observers
   e) computer-assisted test administrators

Thought Questions

1. The state of the subject may well affect his or her test performance and may be a serious source of error. Discuss some possible "subject variables" that may interfere with or improve an individual's performance on a test. (page 187)

2. Explain some ways in which test administration can be standardized. (pages 184-187)

Answers

Terms, Concepts, and Names

expectancy effects (p. 181)
Rosenthal effect (p.181)
reactivity (p.187)
drift (p.188)
partial correlation (p.189)

Fill-in Questions

1. nonverbal communication (p.181)
2. standardized conditions (p.184)
3. test anxiety, subject variable (p.187)
4. reactivity (p.187)

Multiple-Choice Questions

1. e (p. 179)
2. b (p.184)
3. a (p.186)
4. d (p.188)

Chapter 9

Introduction to Applied Aspects of Testing

Terms, Concepts, and Names

Briefly identify the following:

standardization sample______________________________

____

____

standard administration______________________________

____

____

test battery____

____

____

testing____

____

____

assessment____

____

____

Fill-in Questions

1. A standard administration of a test is necessary in order for a comparison of the resulting test data to the ____________________ to be appropriate.
2. Proper test use is the responsibility of ________________________.
3. The goal of __________ is to evaluate an individual so that he or she can be described in terms of current functioning and also so that predictions can be made concerning future functioning. In order for an assessment procedure to be called a test there must be ____________ ____ ____.
4. The most frequently referenced projective personality test is the __________ and the __________ is the most frequently referenced of all personality tests.

Multiple-Choice Questions

1. Which of the following is **not** necessary to know in order to adequately evaluate a test?
   a) its limitations
   b) the characteristics of the standardization sample
   c) the characteristics of the original test administrators
   d) the types and quality of its reliability and validity
   e) all of the above are necessary

2. Which of the following sources of information would probably **not** be included in a test battery?
   a) an interview
   b) direct observation
   c) input from others in the individual's environment
   d) records of past performance
   e) all of the above may be included in a test battery

3. One of the most frequently used and researched intelligence tests is the
   a) Stanford-Binet
   b) Wechsler Intelligence Scales
   c) Buros Mental Measurement Scale
   d) both a and b
   e) both b and c

Thought Question

1. Describe factors which determine the quality of a test (e.g., psychometric properties) and discuss their importance relative to proper test use. What other factors might you want to consider before using a test to make a decision which could affect an individual's life in significant ways? (pages 194-196; also see chapters 4, 5, and 6)

____

____

____

____

____

____

Answers

Terms, Concepts, and Names

standardization sample (p.195)
standard administration (p.195)
test battery (p.197)
testing (p.197)
assessment (p.197)

Fill-in Questions

1. standardization sample (p.195)
2. all concerned; i.e., the test developer, administrator, counselor, teacher, etc. (p. 196)
3. assessment; standard procedures for administration, scoring, and interpretation, a normative sample, and evidence of reliability and validity (p.197)
4. Rorschach, MMPI (p.199)

Multiple-Choice Questions

1. c (p.196)
2. e (p. 197)
3. d (p.199)

Chapter 10

Interview Techniques

Terms, Concepts, and Names

Briefly identify the following:

social facilitation

judgmental statements

probing statements

false reassurance

open-ended question

closed-ended question

transitional phrase

verbatim playback

paraphrase

clarification statement

empathy response

active listening

confrontation____
____
____

halo effect____
____
____

general standoutishness__________________________________
____
____

nonverbal communication_________________________________
____
____

Fill-in Questions

1. A study by Saccuzzo (1975) indicated that the patient's perceptions of the interviewer's __________ were the most important factor in the patient's evaluations of the quality of the interview.
2. __________ statements tend to put the interviewee on guard thus limiting his or her ease in revealing important information.
3. __________ statements demand more information than the interviewee is willing to provide voluntarily and should also be avoided. Many of these statements begin with __________ and tend to put the individual on the defensive.
4. The __________ response directs anger toward the interviewee.
5. __________ questions facilitate the interviewing process, while __________ questions bring the interview to a halt.
6. __________ and __________ help to keep the interview flowing and are interchangeable with the interviewee's response.
7. A powerful response that communicates that the interviewer understands how the interviewee must feel is the __________ response.
8. A confrontation response is used most appropriately in a(n)__________ interview.
9. The __________ interview often involves a search for negative or unfavorable evidence about the person.
10. The reliability of interview data centers around ________________ ________________.
11. Very often __________ behavior is a more accurate reflection of an individual's feelings than __________ behavior.

Multiple-Choice Questions

1. "Don't worry everything will be alright" is an example of
   a) an empathic response
   b) a facilitative response
   c) a confrontive response
   d) an effective response
   e) a response to be avoided

2. What two types of statements go just beyond the interviewee's response?
   a) clarification and transition
   b) clarification and summarizing
   c) clarification and verbatim playback
   d) summarizing and paraphrasing
   e) paraphrasing and restatement

3. Within Carkhuff and Berenson's 5-point system, what is the minimum level of responding necessary to facilitate an interaction?
   a) III
   b) I
   c) II
   d) V
   e) all of the above

4. A special type of interview used primarily to diagnose psychosis, brain damage, and other major mental health problems is the
   a) evaluation interview
   b) assessment interview
   c) case history interview
   d) mental status exam
   e) employment interview

5. Interpretation and analysis of "resistances" characterize the
   a) client-centered approach
   b) psychoanalytic approach
   c) behavioral approach
   d) directive approach
   e) none of the above

6. The PONS test has been used extensively for
   a) research on interviewer bias
   b) improving interviewee responses
   c) research on the halo effect
   d) evaluating and training professionals involved in therapeutic interviews
   e) improving communications within organizations

Thought Questions

1. Describe the 5-point system of Carkhuff and Berenson which represents varying degrees of empathy, and provide examples of each response level. (pages 212-214)

2. Choose a theoretical orientation from amomg those described on pages 218-220 of your text and describe how you might conduct an initial interview from within this framework. Use additional sources as needed.

Answers

Terms, Concepts, and Names

social facilitation (p.205)
judgmental statements (p. 207)
probing statements (p.207)
false reassurance (p. 208)
open-ended question (p. 208)
closed-ended question (p.208)
transitional phrase (p.209)

verbatim playback (p. 210)
paraphrase (p.210)
clarification statement (p.210)
empathy response (p. 211)
active listening (p. 214)
confrontation (p.214)
halo effect (p.221)
general standoutishness (p. 222)
nonverbal communication (p. 223)

<u>Fill-in Questions</u>

1. feelings (p.206)
2. judgmental/evaluative (p.207)
3. probing, why (p.207)
4. hostile (p. 207)
5. open-ended, closed-ended (p.208)
6. paraphrase, restatement (p.210)
7. empathy/understanding (p.211)
8. therapeutic (p.214)
9. employment (p.217)
10. interinterviewer agreement (p.222)
11. nonverbal, verbal (p.224)

<u>Multiple-Choice Questions</u>

1. e (p.208)
2. b (p.210)
3. a (p.213)
4. d (p.216)
5. b (p.219)
6. d (p.224)

Chapter 11

Tests of Mental Ability: The Binet Scale

Terms, Concepts, and Names

Briefly identify the following:

auto criticism____

age differentiation____

general mental ability____

Spearman's *g*____

positive manifold____

1905 Binet-Simon Scale____

1908 Binet-Simon Scale____

mental age____

L. M. Terman____

1916 Stanford-Binet Scale____

intelligence quotient (IQ)____

1937 Stanford-Binet Scale____

deviation IQ____

inherited validity____

1960 Stanford-Binet Scale____

1972 Stanford-Binet Scale____

The Modern Binet Scale____

basal____

ceiling____

primary mental abilities____

Fill-in Questions

1. Rather than attempting to measure separate distinct abilities, Alfred Binet restricted his task to the measurement of ________________.
2. The terms __________, __________, and __________ were used to designate levels of mental deficiency in the early versions of the Binet Scale.
3. The 1908 Scale retained and expanded upon the principle of age differentiation and was a(n) __________ scale.
4. Although the standardization sample of the 1916 Scale was markedly increased it was not ______________.
5. If an eight year old child has a mental age of ten his or her IQ would be computed to be __________.

6. The most important improvement in the 1937 Scale was the inclusion of a(n) ___________________.
7. The single most important psychometric problem of the 1937 Scale was the differential variability in IQ scores as a function of ___________ ___________.
8. In 1960, the __________ concept replaced the original IQ concept and is a standard score with a mean of __________ and a standard deviation of __________.
9. Unlike previous normative samples, the 1972 revised norms included __________.
10. The test format of the Modern (1986) Binet is __________, meaning that each individual is tested with a range of tasks best suited to his or her ability.

Multiple-Choice Questions

1. Binet's definition of intelligence combined one's capacity to (1) find and maintain a definite direction and purpose, (2) adjust strategy if necessary to achieve that purpose, and (3)
   a) reach one's goal
   b) evaluate or criticize the strategy so that necessary adjustments can be made
   c) teach one's strategies to others
   d) be creative in choosing one's strategies
   e) none of the above

2. The first version of what is now referred to as the Stanford-Binet, the Binet-Simon Scale, was developed in
   a) 1905
   b) 1904
   c) 1916
   d) 1927
   e) 1960

3. The 30 items in the Binet-Simon Scale were arranged
   a) according to type of task
   b) randomly to avoid ordering effects
   c) according to underlying ability tapped
   d) in an increasing order of difficulty
   e) none of the above

4. On the Modern Binet Scale, the point at which three out of four items within a test are missed is called the
   a) criterion
   b) mental age
   c) ceiling
   d) level of general capability
   e) floor

5. The 1916 Stanford-Binet was developed under the direction of
   a) T. Simon
   b) J. P. Herring
   c) F. Kuhlman
   d) R. M. Yerkes
   e) L. M. Terman

6. The formula for computing the intelligence quotient (IQ) is
   a) IQ= Chronological age/Mental age x 100 (IQ=CA/MA x 100)
   b) IQ= Basal age/Mental age x 100 (IQ=BA/MA x 100)
   c) IQ= 100/Chronological age x Mental age (IQ=100/CA x MA)
   d) IQ= Mental age/Chronological age x 100 (IQ=MA/CA x 100)
   e) IQ= Chronological age/Basal age x 100 (IQ=CA/BA x 100)

7. A major problem with the Modern Binet is
   a) its inadequate documentation of validity
   b) its cumbersome administration
   c) its poor overall reliability
   d) its small standardization sample
   e) that its norms do not include ethnic minorities

Thought Questions

1. What was the initial impetus for the development of the Stanford-Binet Intelligence Scale? Are intelligence tests still used for this purpose? Describe other possible uses for tests such as the Binet in contemporary society. (page 231)

____
____
____
____
____
____
____
____

2. Discuss Binet's concept of general mental ability in terms of the possible advantages and disadvantages of utilizing such an approach in the measurement of intelligence. (pages 229-231)

Answers

Terms, Concepts, and Names

auto criticism (p.228)
age differentiation (p.229)
general mental ability (p.229)
Spearman's *g* (p.230)
positive manifold (p.230)
1905 Binet-Simon Scale (p.231)
1908 Binet-Simon Scale (p.232)
mental age (p.234)
L. M. Terman (p.235)
1916 Stanford-Binet Scale (p.235)
intelligence quotient (p.236)
1937 Scale (p.237)
1960 Scale (p.239)
deviation IQ (p. 241)
inherited validity (p.241)
1972 Scale (p.241)
Modern Binet Scale (p. 242)
basal (p.243)
ceiling (p.243)
primary mental abilities (p. 245)

Fill-in Questions

1. general mental ability (p.229)
2. idiot, imbecile, moron (p.231)
3. age (p.232)
4. representative (p.236)
5. 125 (pp.236-237)
6. alternate equivalent form (p.238)
7. age of subject (p.238)
8. deviation IQ, 100, 16 (p.241)
9. non-whites (p.241)
10. adaptive (p.243)

Multiple-Choice Questions

1. b (p.228)
2. a (p.231)
3. d (p.231)
4. c (p.243)
5. e (p.235)
6. d (p.236)
7. b (p.248)

Chapter 12

The Wechsler Intelligence Scales

Terms, Concepts, and Names

Briefly identify the following:

point scale____

performance scale__________________________________

Wechsler Adult Intelligence Scale-Revised (WAIS-R)____________

verbal subtests____________________________________

scaled score______________________________________

performance subtests_______________________________

pattern analysis___________________________________

Wechsler Intelligence Scale for Children-R (WISC-R)____________

Wechsler Preschool and Primary Scale of Intelligence (WPPSI)________

Fill-in Questions

1. A major criticism of the Binet Scale made by Wechsler (1939) was _____ ____.
2. An important difference between the Wechsler and Binet scales is that the Binet employs a(n) _______________ concept while the

Wechsler tests use a(n) _____________ concept.

3. In a point scale credits or points are assigned to each item and items can be grouped together according to _________.
4. While Binet set out to measure the concept of general mental ability, Wechsler made an effort to measure ______________________.
5. The ________ subtest taps one of the most stable and best single measures of intelligence.
6. Raw scores on the WAIS-R subtests are converted into scaled scores with a mean of __________ and a standard deviation of _________.
7. To obtain a verbal IQ the _______________ on each of the verbal subtests are __________.
8. The Wechsler Preschool and Primary Scale of Intelligence (WPPSI) measures intelligence in individuals from __________ to __________ years old.
9. __________ is a supplementary subtest found on the Wechsler Intelligence Scale for Children-R (WISC-R) but not on the Wechsler Adult Intelligence Scale-R (WAIS-R).
10. The three unique subtests included in the WPPSI are _______________, _______________, and _______________.

Multiple-Choice Questions

1. The main reason for including a performance scale in a measure of intelligence is to
   a) facilitate scoring
   b) increase ease of administration
   c) improve examiner-examinee rapport
   d) overcome language, cultural, and educational factors
   e) assist the examiner in determining the appropriate level at which to begin testing

2. Which of the following is **not** one of the WAIS-R performance scales?
   a) object assembly
   b) block design
   c) arithmetic
   d) picture completion
   e) digit symbol

3. The major function measured by the comprehension subtest is
   a) judgment
   b) memory
   c) abstract thinking
   d) range of knowledge
   e) concentration

4. Alertness to details is best measured by the
   a) object assembly subtest
   b) picture completion subtest
   c) digit symbol subtest
   d) picture arrangement subtest
   e) similarities subtest

5. The performance IQ has a mean and standard deviation of
   a) 100, 15
   b) 10, 3
   c) 100, 10
   d) 100, 3
   e) 10, 5

6. One criticism of the WAIS-R is
   a) its weakness in measuring verbal abilities
   b) its poor reliability
   c) its poor validity
   d) its poor norms and standardization
   e) its weakness in measuring extreme IQs

7. Which of the following is **not** a weakness of the WISC-R?
   a) poor reliability coefficients for the verbal, performance, and full scale IQ scores
   b) it does not take into account more recent theories of multiple intelligences
   c) it lacks treatment validity for children with specific academic deficiencies
   d) it contains problems of bias for certain cultural and racial groups
   e) all of the above are weaknesses of the WISC-R

<u>Thought Questions</u>

1. On pages 256-257 of your text there are figures which describe both intellective and non-intellective components of the Information and

Arithmetic subtests. Choose another subtest and discuss in a similar fashion possible factors that may influence an individual's performance. (pages 255-263)

2. Discuss both the advantages and disadvantages of the Wechsler Scales as compared to the Modern Binet Scale. (pages 252-270)

Answers

Terms, Concepts and Names

point scale (p.252)
performance scale (p.253)
Wechsler Adult Intelligence Scale-Revised (WAIS-R) (p. 254)
verbal subtests (pp. 255-258)
scaled score (pp. 258-260)
performance subtests (pp. 261-263)
pattern analysis (p.264)
Wechsler Intelligence Scale for Children-R (WISC-R) (p.270)
Wechsler Preschool and Primary Scale of Intelligence (WPPSI) (p.274)

Fill-in Questions

1. the inappropriateness of the Binet Scale as a measure of adult intelligence (p.252)
2. age scale, point scale (p.252)
3. content (p.253)
4. separate interrelated abilities (p.255)
5. vocabulary (p.258)
6. 10, 3 (p.259)
7. scaled scores, summed (p.260)
8. 4, 6 1/2 (p.274)
9. mazes (p.271)
10. animal house, geometric design, sentences (p.274)

Multiple-Choice Questions

1. d (p.253)
2. c (p.255)
3. a (p.255)
4. b (p.255)
5. a (p.263)
6. e (p.269)
7. a (p.269)

Chapter 13

Other Individual Tests of Ability

Terms, Concepts, and Names

Briefly identify the following:

Seguin Form Board Test

Brazelton Neonatal Assessment Scale

Gesell Developmental Schedules

developmental quotient

Bayley Scales of Infant Development

Cattell Infant Intelligence Scale

McCarthy Scales of Children's Abilities

general cognitive index

Kaufman Assessment Battery for Children (K-ABC)

Columbia Mental Maturity Scale

age deviation score

Peabody Picture Vocabulary Test______________________________________

____

____

Leiter International Performance Scale_______________________________

____

____

Porteus Maze Test____

____

____

Illinois Test of Psycholinguistic Abilities___________________________

____

____

human information processing___________________________________

____

____

Benton Visual Retention Test____________________________________

____

____

psychological deficit____

____

____

Bender Visual Motor Gestalt Test_________________________________

____

____

Memory for Designs Test_______________________________________

____

____

Torrance Tests of Creative Thinking_______________________________

____

____

Wide Range Achievement Test___________________________________

____

____

Fill-in Questions

1. Although usually weaker in terms of psychometric properties, many of the alternatives to the major scales are not as reliant on a(n) __________ as are the Binet and Wechsler Scales.
2. The Seguin Form Board Test was used primarily to________________ and emphasized ____________________.
3. The major limitation of the Brazelton Scale is its ________________.
4. The Bayley Scale produces two main scores: __________ and

________.

5. The ____________________ was designed as a downward extension of the Stanford-Binet.
6. The __________________ yield(s) a composite score known as the general cognitive index.
7. The Kaufman Assessment Battery for Children (K-ABC) is based on a combination of several theoretical approaches including Luria's neuropsychological model of brain functioning, the theory of split brain functioning, and theories of _________________.
8. One of the distinguishing characteristics of the Columbia Mental Maturity Scale is that it requires neither a(n) ________________ nor ____________________.
9. The Peabody Picture Vocabulary Test purports to measure ____________________ which is presumed to be a nonverbal estimate of verbal intelligence.
10. The ____________________ is a test for individual's 2-18 years of age, can be administered without the use of language, and requires no verbal response from subjects.
11. The Illinois Test of Psycholinguistic Abilities assumes that a human response to an outside stimulus can be viewed in terms of discrete stages or processes. Stage 2 of processing involves ________________ ______________________.
12. The idea behind the ____________________ is that a deficit on a visual memory task is consistent with possible brain damage.
13. Errors on the Bender Visual Motor Gestalt Test can occur for individuals whose mental age is less than 8, __________________, and _________________________.

Multiple-Choice Questions

1. Which of the following is **not** a difference among the alternatives to the major scales?
   a) the degree of psychometric superiority as compared to the Wechsler or Binet Scales
   b) the age range
   c) the type of score that results
   d) the type of response required
   e) the amount of examiner skill and experience necessary administration

2. The developmental quotient (DQ) is employed in the
   a) Brazelton Neonatal Assessment Scale

b) Bayley Scales of Infant Development
c) Gesell Developmental Schedules
d) Cattell Infant Intelligence Scale
e) Kaufman Assessment Battery for Children

3. The developmental quotient (DQ) parallels the
   a) chronological age (CA) concept
   b) intelligence quotient (IQ) concept
   c) general cognitive index (GCI) concept
   d) mental age (MA) concept
   e) age deviation score (ADS) concept

4. Which of the following tests seems to be a good predictor for handicapped populations but does not predict future intelligence within the normal ranges?
   a) Bayley Scales of Infant Development
   b) Cattell Infant Intelligence Scale
   c) Gesell Developmental Schedules
   d) Brazelton Neonatal Assessment Scale
   e) McCarthy Scales of Children's Abilities

5. The greatest difficulty with the Columbia Mental Maturity Scale in its present form is its
   a) poor standardization sample
   b) high vulnerability to random error
   c) poor test-retest reliability
   d) poor internal consistency
   e) both a and b

6. Which of the following is a procedure with relevance for assessing brain damage?
   a) Leiter International Performance Scale
   b) Illinois Test of Psycholinguistic Abilities
   c) Porteus Maze Test
   d) Bender Visual Motor Gestalt Test
   e) Columbia Mental Maturity Scale

Thought Questions

1. In previous chapters both Binet's (Chapter 11) and Wechsler's (Chapter 12) definitions of intelligence were presented. In the current chapter a

somewhat different description of intelligence is given. Compare and contrast the definitions of McCarthy, Binet, and Wechsler. (page 289)

2. Utilize the brief description of information processing theory found on pages 300-301 of your text in providing examples of how deficits at each of the three stages may interfere with performance. Also, discuss how impairments in each of the sensory modalities (i.e., visual, auditory, tactile) may impair learning.

Answers

Terms, Concepts, and Names

Seguin Form Board Test (p.281)
Brazelton Neonatal Assessment Scale (p.281)
Gesell Developmental Schedules (p.283)
developmental quotient (DQ) (p.283)
Bayley Scales of Infant Development (p.285)
Cattell Infant Intelligence Scale (p. 286)
McCarthy Scales of Childrens's Abilities (p.289)
general cognitive index (p.289)
Kaufman Assessment Battery for Children (K-ABC) (p.291)
Columbia Mental Maturity Scale (p.295)
age deviation score (p.296)
Peabody Picture Vocabulary Test (p.297)
Leiter International Performance Scale (p.298)
Porteus Maze Test (p.299)
Illinois Test of Psycholinguistic Abilities (p.300)
human information processing (p.300)
Benton Visual Retention Test (p.302)
psychological deficit (p.302)
Bender Visual Motor Gestalt Test (p.302)
Memory for Designs Test (p.303)
Torrance Tests of Creative Thinking (p.304)
Wide Range Achievement Test (p.304)

Fill-in Questions

1. verbal response (p.278)
2. evaluate mentally retarded adults, speed of performance (p.281)
3. lack of normative data (p.282)
4. mental, motor (p.285)
5. Cattell Infant Intelligence Scale (p.286)
6. McCarthy Scales of Children's Abilities (p.289)
7. information processing theory (p.293)
8. verbal response, fine motor skills (p.296)
9. receptive vocabulary (p.297)
10. Leiter International Performance Scale (p.298)
11. analyzing or processing input information (p.301)
12. Benton Visual Retention Test (p.302)
13. individuals with organicity, individuals with emotional problems (p.303)

Multiple-Choice Questions

1. a (p.279)
2. c (p.283)
3. d (p.283)
4. a (p.286)
5. b (p.297)
6. d (p.302)

Chapter 14

Group Ability Tests: Intelligence, Achievement, and Aptitude

Terms, Concepts, and Names

Briefly identify the following:

individual test____

group test____

Kuhlmann-Anderson Test (KAT)______________________________

Henmon-Nelson Test (H-NT)______________________________

Cognitive Abilities Test (COGAT)____________________________

Developing Cognitive Abilities Test (DCAT)____________________

Scholastic Aptitude Test (SAT)____________________________

Cooperative School and College Ability Tests (SCAT)_____________

Graduate Record Examination Aptitude Test (GRE)_______________

Miller Analogies Test (MAT)______________________________

Raven Progressive Matrices (RPM)__________________________

Goodenough-Harris Drawing Test ______________________________

____

____

IPAT Culture Fair Intelligence Test____________________________

____

____

Wonderlic Personnel Test (WPT)______________________________

____

____

Armed Services Vocational Aptitude Battery (ASVAB)______________

____

____

Fill-in Questions

1. Individual tests require a(n) __________ examiner for a(n) __________ subject. Group tests, on the other hand, can be administered to ____________________ at the same time by a(n) ____________________.
2. With __________ tests subjects record their own responses but with __________ tests the examiner scores the subject's response.
3. The ____________________ test provides three separate scores; Verbal, Quantitative, and Nonverbal.
4. The purpose of the ____________________ test is to provide a quick measure of general intelligence.
5. The SAT yields two main scores: a(n) __________ score and a(n) __________ score.
6. The major assumption of the SCAT is that ____
7. The GRE contains a general section that produces __________, __________, and __________ scores.
8. The Raven Progressive Matrices was initially designed to assess military recruits independently of ____________________.
9. Scoring of the Goodenough-Harris Drawing Test follows the principle of ____________________.
10. The Armed Services Vocational Aptitude Battery (ASVAB) uses _______________ which involves presenting an item of known

difficulty and then presenting either a more difficult or a less difficult item depending on whether the test taker is correct.

Multiple-Choice Questions

1. Which of the following is **not** an advantage of group tests?
   a) they are more cost-efficient
   b) they provide a greater wealth of information about the subject
   c) they require less professional time
   d) they require less skill in and training of examiners
   e) they can be scored more objectively

2. It is best to refer the subject for individual testing when
   a) he or she receives a low score
   b) there are wide discrepancies between a test score and other sources of data
   c) the test may not be valid
   d) both b and c
   e) all of the above

3. Unlike most multilevel batteries the Kuhlmann-Anderson Test
   a) is primarily nonverbal
   b) is for individuals from first through twelfth grade
   c) has poor norms
   d) is difficult to administer
   e) all of the above

4. A major weakness of the SAT is its
   a) poor validity documentation
   b) poor predictive power in discriminating the grades of students who score between 900 and 1200
   c) low reliability coefficients
   d) inadequate norms
   e) both c and d

5. A score of 600 on the verbal section of the GRE would mean that the individual scored
   a) at the mean
   b) one standard deviation below the mean
   c) one standard deviation above the mean
   d) two standard deviations above the mean
   e) two standard deviations below the mean

6. Although adequate psychometrically, both the Miller Analogies Test and the GRE have rather poor
   a) construct validity
   b) internal consistency
   c) test-retest reliability
   d) predictive validity
   e) face validity

7. The biggest problem(s) with the Progressive Matrices Test is (are) the
   a) lack of United States norms
   b) poor reliability
   c) problems with the test manual
   d) both a and b
   e) both a and c

Thought Questions

1. Your text outlines both some of the advantages and disadvantages of using the GRE as a means for selecting graduate students. Discuss these arguments and provide your own additional comments regarding the use and misuse of the GRE as a selection device. (pages 318-322)

2. As mentioned in your text, one purpose of nonverbal and performance tests is to remove factors related to cultural influences so that pure intelligence can be measured. Discuss the types of factors one would want to eliminate and the likelihood of being able to do so. (page 325)

Answers

Terms, Concepts, and Names

individual test (pp. 307-309)
group test (pp. 307-312)
Kuhlman-Anderson Test (KAT) (p.312)
Henmon-Nelson Test (H-NT) (p.313)
Cognitive Abilities Test (COGAT) (p.314)
Developing Cognitive Abilities Test (DCAT) (p. 315)
Scholastic Aptitude Test (SAT) (p.316)
Cooperative School and College Ability Tests (SCAT) (p.318)
Graduate Record Examination Aptitude Test (GRE) (p.318)

Miller Analogies Test (MAT) (p.322)
Raven Progressive Matrices (RPM) (p.324)
Goodenough-Harris Drawing Test (p.325)
IPAT Culture Fair Intelligence Test (p.325)
Wonderlic Personnel Test (WPT) (p.326)
Armed Services Vocational Aptitude Battery (ASVAB) (p.327)

Fill-in Questions

1. single, single, more than one person, single examiner (pp.307-308)
2. group, individual (p.308)
3. Cognitive Abilities Test (p.314)
4. Henmon-Nelson Test (p.313)
5. verbal, mathematical (p.316)
6. previous success in acquiring school-learned abilities can predict future success in acquiring such abilities (p.318)
7. verbal, quantitative, reasoning (p.318)
8. educational factors (p.324)
9. age differentiation (p.325)
10. adaptive testing (p.328)

Multiple-Choice Questions

1. b (p.309)
2. e (p.311)
3. a (p.312)
4. b (p.317)
5. c (p.319)
6. d (p.323)
7. e (p.324)

Chapter 15

Tests for Choosing Careers

Terms, Concepts, and Names

Briefly identify the following:

Strong Vocational Interest Blank (SVIB)____________________________

Strong-Campbell Interest Inventory (SCII)__________________________

Kuder Occupational Interest Survey (KOIS)_________________________

Minnesota Vocational Interest Inventory (MVII)______________________

Career Assessment Inventory ____________________________________

self-directed search____

Samuel Osipow____

Donald Super____

vocational maturity____

Anne Roe____

attribution theory____

social ecology______________________________

checklists______________________________

critical incidents______________________________

observation______________________________

interviews______________________________

questionnaires______________________________

template-matching technique______________________________

attitude______________________________

Likert format______________________________

Thurstone format______________________________

Fill-in Questions

1. The Strong Vocational Interest Blank (SVIB) was created using the ____________________ approach to test construction.
2. In addition to suggesting which occupational group might be best suited to a test taker's interests, the Kuder Occupational Interest Survey (KOIS) may also provide direction with regard to ______________________________.
3. The __________________ is designed for individuals who are not oriented toward college and emphasizes skilled and semi-skilled trades.
4. Because it was designed for non-professionally oriented adults and avoids both cultural and sex biases, the _________________ has been

considered the working person's Strong-Campbell Interest Inventory (SCII).

5. Vocational maturity refers to the correspondence between _______________ and the _______________ for that age period.

6. The _________________________ was developed to measure the characteristics described by Roe's theory including person versus nonperson orientation.

7. Attribution theorists posit that events in a person's environment can be caused by one of three sources: __________, __________, and __________.

8. According to attribution theory, when we are observers making judgements about other people we use __________ explanations. On the other hand, when we are the actors in a situation we explain our behavior in terms of __________.

9. One of the most important areas in social ecology is the study of _____________________.

10. Information gathered through observation may be biased since people change their behavior when they know they are being watched. To avoid this problem the ____________________ method is sometimes used.

11. In constructing a Likert scale for attitude measurement, the researcher must be sure that the scale is ___________.

12. __________ methods are used to estimate how a larger group would respond on the basis of interviews from a smaller sample.

Multiple-Choice Questions

1. A major improvement of the Strong-Campbell Interest Inventory (SCII) over the Strong Vocational Interest Blank (SVIB) was/were
   a) an incorporation of a theoretical base
   b) an increase in test-retest reliability
   c) scales devoid of sex bias
   d) both a and b
   e) both a and c

2. Which of the following is **not** one of Holland's six personality factors incorporated into the Strong-Campbell Interest Inventory?
   a) Realistic
   b) Artistic
   c) Intuitive
   d) Social
   e) Enterprising

3. Both the Strong-Campbell Interest Inventory and the Kuder Occupational Interest Survey have been criticized because
   a) they emphasize professions that require college educations
   b) they are strongly sex biased
   c) their predictive validity is questionable
   d) their reliability documentation is poor
   e) interpretation of scores is difficult

4. A theory of career choice which states that individuals go through five developmental stages leading to vocational maturity was proposed by
   a) Donald Super
   b) D. P. Campbell
   c) Samuel Osipow
   d) Anne Roe
   e) E. K. Strong

5. Which of the following methods of job analysis involves the observation of behaviors that differentiate successful from unsuccessful employees?
   a) checklists
   b) observation
   c) questionnaires
   d) critical incidents
   e) interviews

Thought Questions

1. Some general issues in the measurement of interests are described in your text on pages 343-345. Discuss how, in your opinion, faking, sex bias, and a mismatching between abilities and interests may interfere with the reliability and validity of interest inventories.

____
____
____
____
____
____
____
____

2. Utilize the discussion of attribution theory found on pages 348-349 of your text to describe why a particular event in your environment took place or is taking place. This can be an event in which you are the "actor" or the "observer."

3. Describe the characteristics of a behavioral setting of interest and include some of the "rules" which govern this particular setting. (pages 349-350)

Answers

Terms, Concepts, and Names

Strong Vocational Interest Blank (SVIB) (p.331)
Strong-Campbell Interest Inventory (SCII) (p.332)
Kuder Occupational Interest Survey (KOIS) (p.335)
Minnesota Vocational Interest Inventory (MVII) (p.342)
Career Assessment Inventory (p.342)
self-directed search (p.343)
Samuel Osipow (p.345)
Donald Super (p.346)
vocational maturity (p.346)
Anne Roe (p.346)
attribution theory (p.348)
social ecology (p.349)
checklists (p.353)
critical incidents (p.354)
observation (p.354)
interviews (p.354)
questionnaires (p.354)
template-matching technique (p.357)
attitude (p.358)
Likert format (p.358)
Thurstone format (p.358)

Fill-in Questions

1. criterion-keying/criterion group (p.331)
2. selection of a college major (p.335)
3. Minnesota Vocational Interest Inventory (MVII) (p.342)
4. Career Assessment Inventory (p.342)
5. vocational behavior, expected behavior (p.346)
6. California Occupational Preference Survey (p.346)
7. persons, entities, times (p.348)
8. trait, situations (pp. 348-349)
9. behavioral settings (p.349)
10. participant observation (p.354)
11. uni-dimensional (p.358)
12. Survey (p.359)

Multiple-Choice Questions

1. e (p.332)
2. c (p.333)
3. a (p.342)
4. a (p.346)
5. d (p.354)

Chapter 16

Structured Personality Tests

Terms, Concepts, and Names

Briefly identify the following:

self-report questionnaire________________________

structured/objective method of personality assessment____________

deductive strategies________________________

logical-content strategy________________________

theoretical strategy________________________

empirical strategies________________________

criterion group strategy________________________

external criterion________________________

factor analytic strategy________________________

Woodworth Personal Data Sheet________________________

Bell Adjustment Inventory________________________

Bernreuter Personality Inventory________________________

Mooney Problem Checklist____
____
____

Minnesota Multiphasic Personality Inventory (MMPI)______________
____
____

California Psychological Inventory (CPI)__________________________
____
____

J. P. Guilford____
____
____

R. B. Cattell____
____
____

Sixteen Personality Factor Questionnaire (16PF)__________________
____
____

Edwards Personal Preference Schedule (EPPS)______________________
____
____

ipsative score____
____
____

Personality Research Form (PRF)___________________________________
____
____

Fill-in Questions

1. The principal distinguishing characteristic of the logical-content strategy is that it assumes that the test item ______________________ ____.
2. The theoretical approach attempts to create a __________ scale.
3. When employing the criterion group strategy the first step is to determine which items discriminate the criterion and control groups. The next step is to ____________________ the scale.
4. Factor analysts analyze intercorrelations among items or tests in order to find the minimum number of areas of ____________________ to account for as much of the variability in the data as possible.

5. The purpose of the Woodworth Personal Data Sheet was to ___________
____.

6. Items on the Mooney Problem Checklist are interpreted on the basis of _______________.

7. The logical-content approach has been criticized because in assuming the face validity of test items one also assumes that the subject takes a normal approach to the test, ___________________________, ___________________, and ____________________.

8. The main idea behind the MMPI was to _____________________________
____.

9. The __________ scale(s) of the MMPI provide information concerning the subject's approach to testing.

10. The authors of the MMPI were _______________, a psychologist, and _______________, a physician.

11. The __________ scale was designed to identify individuals who attempt to fake bad.

12. Using two-point codes and other configural patterns ___________ attempted to empirically determine the meaning of MMPI elevations.

13. Name two psychometric inadequacies of the MMPI. _____________
____.

14. __________ is a response style which is a tendency to agree or to endorse an item as true.

15. Cattell, through a series of factor analyses, reduced personality traits to 16 basic dimensions which he called ________________.

16. One major criticism of the factor analytic approach is ___________
_____________________________________.

17. Each score on any given set of tests or variables can be broken down into three components: _______________, _______________, and ____________________.

18. Ipsative scores present results in _______________ rather than as absolute totals.

19. Both the EPPS and the PRF were based on _______________________.

Multiple-Choice Questions

1. The two deductive strategies of test construction are the
    a) logical content and rational approaches
    b) logical content and empirical approaches
    c) logical content and theoretical approaches
    d) empirical and rational approaches
    e) intuitive and rational approaches

2. The criterion group strategy is also known as the
   a) empirical strategy
   b) external strategy
   c) factor analytic strategy
   d) both a and b
   e) both b and c

3. The Bell Adjustment Inventory is an example of
   a) the theoretical approach
   b) the criterion group approach
   c) the empirical approach
   d) the logical-content approach
   e) the factor analytic approach

4. The MMPI consists of how many validity and clinical scales respectively?
   a) 3, 10
   b) 5, 10
   c) 10, 10
   d) 5, 15
   e) 4, 10

5. Raw scores on the MMPI are converted to standardized scores called
   a) Z-scores
   b) V-scores
   c) T-scores
   d) C-scores
   e) K-scores

6. Which MMPI scale was designed to detect pathological individuals who produce normal patterns because of defensiveness?
   a) L scale
   b) K scale
   c) F scale
   d) Si scale
   e) D scale

7. The restandardization of the MMPI has eliminated the most serious drawback of the original version, namely
   a) an inadequate control group
   b) lack of validity documentation
   c) poor reliability
   d) inter-item correlations
   e) poor predictive ability for certain ethnic groups

8. A number of studies have indicated that the MMPI might be useful in the early detection of individuals who later become
   a) rapists
   b) child molesters
   c) physically ill
   d) obese
   e) alcoholics

9. The advantage of the CPI over the MMPI is that
   a) there is no intercorrelation among scales
   b) it can be used with normal subjects
   c) true-false keying is balanced to prevent response bias
   d) reliability coefficients are impressive
   e) criterion groups were carefully and accurately selected

10. The EPPS exemplifies which of the following approaches to test construction?
   a) the factor analytic strategy
   b) the criterion group strategy
   c) the criterion-keying method
   d) the logical-content approach
   e) the theoretical strategy

11. Which of the following tests is characterized by a forced-choice format?
   a) EPPS
   b) 16PF
   c) CPI
   d) MMPI
   e) PRF

Thought Questions

1. Select one of the approaches to test construction described on pages 364-367 of your text and discuss both the advantages and disadvantages of this strategy for personality test construction. What modifications might you make to improve on this approach?

____

____

____

____

2. The measurement of personality assumes that humans possess characteristics or traits that are stable across situations, vary from individual to individual, and can be measured. Discuss these assertions and your agreement and/or disageement with them as well as possible alternative assumptions; for example, situational variables. (page 379)

Answers

Terms, Concepts, and Names

self-report questionnaire (p.364)
structured/objective method of personality assessment (p.364)
deductive strategies (p.365)
logical-content strategy (p.365)
theoretical strategy (p.365)
empirical strategies (p.366)
criterion group strategy (p.366)
external criterion (p.366)
factor analytic strategy (p.367)
Woodworth Personal Data Sheet (p.368)
Bell Adjustment Inventory (p.369)
Bernreuter Personality Inventory (p.369)
Mooney Problem Checklist (p.369)
Minnesota Multiphasic Personality Inventory (MMPI) (p.370)
California Pychological Inventory (CPI) (p. 378)
J. P. Guilford (p.380)
R. B. Cattell (p.380)
Sixteen Personality Factor Questionnaire (16PF) (p.381)
Edwards Personal Preference Schedule (EPPS) (p.383)
ipsative score (p.384)
Personality Research Form (PRF) (p. 385)

Fill-in Questions

1. describes the subject's personality and behavior (p.365)
2. homogenous (p.366)
3. cross-validate (p.367)
4. common variance (p.367)
5. identify military recruits likely to break down in combat (p.368)
6. face vailidity (p.370)
7. complies with instructions, reads each item, answers as honestly as possible (p.370)
8. assume nothing about the meaning of a subject's response to a test item (p.370)
9. validity (p.371)
10. S. R. Hathaway, J. C. McKinley (p.372)
11. F Scale (p.373)
12. Paul Meehl (p.374)
13. any two of the following: composition of scales, intercorrelations among the scales, imbalance in the way items are keyed, relationship of demographic characteristics to scales (pp.376-377)
14. Acquiescence (p.377)
15. source traits (p.381)
16. the subjective nature of the process of naming factors (p.382)
17. common variance, unique variance, error variance (p. 382)
18. relative terms (p.384)
19. Murray's (1938) theory of needs (p.385)

Multiple-Choice Questions

1. c (p.365)
2. d (p.366)
3. d (p.369)
4. a (p.371)
5. c (p.371)
6. b (p.373)
7. a (p.378)
8. e (p.378)
9. b (p.379)
10. e (p.383)
11. a (p.383)

Chapter 17

Projective Personality Tests

Terms, Concepts, and Names

Briefly identify the following:

projective hypothesis____

Rorschach Inkblot Test____

Psychodiagnostik____

administration of the Rorschach____

scoring of the Rorschach____

Holtzman Inkblot Test____

Thematic Apperception Test (TAT)____

Southern-Mississippi TAT____

Children's Apperception Test (CAT)____

Gerontological Apperception Test____

Fill-in Questions

1. The projective hypothesis proposes that an individual's interpretation of __________ stimuli tends to reflect his or her ____.

2. Although inkblots had been used previously for a variety of purposes Herman Rorschach found an original and important use for inkblots; ______________________.

3. Exner (1974) advocates an administration procedure in which the examiner sits next to the subject rather than face to face in order to prevent the examiner from ______________________________.
4. The two phases of Rorschach adminstration are the ______________ phase and the __________.
5. In scoring for location a __________ response indicates that the subject overgeneralized from a part to the whole.
6. Four of the properties of an inkblot that may determine or lead to a response are __________, __________, __________, and __________.
7. "Populars" are responses that occur _______________.
8. The specific content of Rorschach responses and an analysis of the sequence of responses are examples of __________ aspects of scoring.
9. Two factors that contribute to the problem of evaluating the psychometric properties of the Rorschach are ______________________________and ______________________________.
10. Although it possesses psychometric advantages over the Rorschach the main problem with the Holtzman Inkblot Test appears to be its ____________.
11. While the Rorschach is basically atheoretical, the Thematic Apperception Test (TAT) is based on __________________.
12. Almost all methods of TAT interpretation take into account __________, __________, __________, __________, and ________.

Multiple-Choice Questions

1. Which of the following is **not** one of the five individuals who originally played a dominant role in the use and investigation of the Rorschach?
   a) Beck
   b) Hertz
   c) Klopfer
   d) Exner
   e) Piotrowski

2. How many Rorschach Inkblot cards are there?
   a) 15
   b) 10
   c) 5
   d) 20
   e) 12

3. The purpose of the second phase of Rorschach adminisration, the inquiry, is to
   a) determine how long it takes a subject to respond to a card
   b) record the position of the card when the response is made
   c) allow the examiner to score the response
   d) check the reliability of the subject's response
   e) both a and b

4. Form quality is a scoring dimension which refers to
   a) where the pereception was seen
   b) what determined the response
   c) the extent to which the response matched the stimulus properties of the inkblot
   d) the extent to which the response was unique
   e) what the perception was

5. A comprehensive system for administering and scoring the Rorschach was developed by
   a) Beck
   b) Hertz
   c) Klopfer
   d) Exner
   e) Piotrowski

6. In TAT interpretation the environmental forces that interfere with or facilitate the satisfaction of various needs are called
   a) press
   b) external stimuli
   c) themes
   d) determinors
   e) stressors

7. A number of assumptions for TAT interpretation were analyzed by
   a) Morgan
   b) Murray
   c) Bellack
   d) Lindzey
   e) Murstein

Thought Questions

1. A summary of arguments for and against the Rorschach is presented in Table 17-2 on page 402 of your text. Discuss these arguments and include your own views regarding the utility of the Rorschach Inkblot Test.

2. Discuss the similarities and differences between the Rorschach Inkblot Test and TAT. (pages 391-403, Rorschach; pages 404-409, TAT)

Answers

Terms, Concepts, and Names

projective hypothesis (p.390)
Rorschach Inkblot Test (p.391)
Psychodiagnostik (p.391)
Rorschach administration (pp. 392-393)
Rorschach scoring (pp. 394-401)
Holtzman Inkblot Test (p.403)
Thematic Apperception Test (TAT) (p.404)
Southern-Mississippi TAT (p.410)
Children's Apperception Test (CAT) (p.410)
Gerontological Apperception Test (p.410)

Fill-in Questions

1. vague/ambiguous; needs, feelings, experiences, prior conditioning, thought processes, etc. (p.390)
2. identifying psychological disorders (p.391)
3. inadvertently revealing information or reinforcing certain types of responses through facial expressions or nonverbal communication (p.393)
4. free association, inquiry (pp.393-394)
5. confabulatory (p.394)
6. form, movement, color, shading (p.395)

7. once in three protocols (p.397)
8. qualitative (p.397)
9. lack of a standard method of administration, lack of standard scoring procedures (p.401)
10. validity (p.404)
11. Murray's (1938) theory of needs (p.404)
12. hero, needs, press, themes, outcomes (p.407)

Multiple-Choice Questions

1. d (p.392)
2. b (p.392)
3. c (p.394)
4. c (p.397)
5. d (p.403)
6. a (p.407)
7. d (p.407)

Chapter 18

Alternatives to Traditional Psychological Tests

Terms, Concepts, and Names

Briefly identify the following:

medical model______________________________________

behavioral assessment__________________________________

operant conditioning___________________________________

baseline____

self-report techniques_________________________________

Fear Survey Schedule (FSS)_____________________________

Assertive Behavior Survey Schedule (ABSS)__________________

Rathus Assertiveness Schedule (RAS)______________________

Conflict Resolution Inventory (CRI)_______________________

self-report battery____________________________________

Kanfer and Saslow's functional approach___________________

cognitive-behavioral assessment

Thought Sampling Questionnaire (TSQ)

Klinger

Meichenbaum

Irrational Beliefs Test (IBT)

cognitive functional analysis

psychophysiological assessment

Azrin and Powell

Ax

artifacts

psychophysical and signal detection procedures

Saccuzzo

iconic storage

Fill-in Questions

1. The medical model assumes that overt manifestations of psychopathology are only __________ of a(n) __________ cause.
2. In behavioral assessment the __________ is(are) considered the real problem.
3. The first step in behavioral assessment based on operant conditioning is to ____.
4. The establishment of a baseline involves an evaluation of the __________, __________, or __________ of the critical response(s).
5. In behavioral terms overeating is an example of a behavioral __________ while undereating is an example of a behavioral __________.
6. An individual's responses to self-report items are assumed to be related to ______________________________________.
7. Behavioral self-report procedures focus on __________ that lead to particular response patterns. Traditional procedures, on the other hand, focus on ______________________________ that lead to particular response patterns.
8. Both early and present-day self-report procedures assume that a test response can be interpreted on the basis of ______________.
9. The focus of Kanfer and Saslow's functional approach is on __________ __________ and ______________.
10. Thought sampling, assessing imagery, assessing beliefs, and assessing self-statements are all examples of ______________________.
11. The premise underlying __________________ is that what an individual says to his or herself plays an important role in behavior.
12. Mechanical counters attached to the jaw that record the number of bites taken while eating and electronic devices attached to cigarette cases which count the number of times it is opened, are examples of ______________________.
13. Saccuzzo and his colleagues have attempted to demonstrate that __________________ may be evaluated by psychophysiological methods.

Multiple-Choice Questions

1. The Fear Survey Schedule (FSS) attempts to identify
   a) those individuals most likely to be fearful in a variety of situations
   b) internal characteristics that lead to fear responses
   c) situations that elicit fear and avoidance

d) how fearful individuals are of a variety of phenomena
e) the circumstances under which typically fearful individuals are the least likely to be afraid

2. Which of the following questionnaires seeks to determine whether or not an individual would comply with a series of unreasonable requests and how he or she would feel about his or her response?
   a) Conflict Resolution Inventory (CRI)
   b) Assertive Behavior Survey Schedule (ABSS)
   c) Fear of Negative Evaluation Scale (FNE)
   d) Rathus Assertiveness Schedule (RAS)
   e) Social Avoidance Distress Scale (SAD)

3. Among the strengths of the Fear Survey Schedule (FSS) which sets it apart from other self-report techniques is its
   a) standardized administration procedure
   b) standardized scoring and interpretation
   c) generalizability to a variety of populations
   d) excellent test-retest reliability
   e) none of the above

4. Which of the following researchers in psychophysiological assessment demonstrated that the fear response was related to specific physiological changes?
   a) Klinger
   b) Meichenbaum
   c) Powell
   d) Ax
   e) Azrin

5. One potential drawback of the computerization of traditional tests is that
   a) there is a significant reduction in reliability
   b) interpretations based on computer programs must be viewed with caution
   c) there are frequent scoring errors
   d) computerized test administration is cumbersome
   e) there is an appreciable decrease in validity

Thought Questions

1. A 40 year old woman has been drinking alcohol excessively for the past 15 years. Her behavior has recently caused her to be fired from her job and is starting to detrimentally affect her relationships with her husband and children. Discuss how you would assess and begin to treat her problem first from a traditional (medical model) perspective and then using an alternative assessment procedure. (pages 415-430)

2. Choose a behavior that you would like to increase or decrease. For example, you may want to eat less, exercise more, increase your study time, or decrease your television watching. The steps outlined in table 18-1 on page 417 of your text may be helpful in planning an intervention. What rewards and/or punishments did you use? How effective was your intervention? The example on pages 416-419 may serve as a useful guideline.

Answers

Terms, Concepts, and Names

- medical model (p.415)
- behavioral assessment (p.415)
- operant conditioning (p.416)
- baseline (p.416)
- self-report techniques (p.419)
- Fear Survey Schedule (FSS) (p.421)
- Assertive Behavior Survey Shedule (ABSS) (p.421)
- Rathus Assertiveness Schedule (RAS) (p.422)
- Conflict Resolution Inventory (CRI) (p.422)
- self-report battery (p.423)

Kanfer and Saslow's functional approach (p.424)
cognitive-behavioral assessment (p.425)
Thought Sampling Questionnaire (TSQ) (p.425)
Klinger (p.425)
Meichenbaum (p.427)
Irrational Beliefs Test (IBT) (p.426)
cognitive functional analysis (p.427)
psychophysiological assessment (p.428)
Azrin and Powell (p.428)
Ax (p.428)
artifacts (p.429)
psychophysical and signal detection procedures (p.430)
Saccuzzo (p.430)
iconic storage (p.431)

Fill-in Questions

1. symptom, underlying (p.415)
2. overt behaviors that define a disordered condition (p.415)
3. identify the critical response involved in the behavior (p.417)
4. frequency, intensity, duration (p.416)
5. excess, deficit (p.416)
6. behavior that can actually be observed (p.419)
7. situations, enduring internal characteristics of the individual (p.420)
8. face validity (p.423)
9. behavioral excesses, behavioral deficits (p.424)
10. cognitive-behavioral assessment (p.425)
11. cognitive functional analysis (p.427)
12. self-monitoring devices (pp. 427-428)
13. psychological disorders (p.430)

Multiple-Choice Questions

1. c (p.421)
2. a (p.422)
3. e (p.423)
4. d (p.428)
5. b (p.433)

Chapter 19

Measures of Anxiety and Stress

Terms, Concepts, and Names:

Briefly identify the following:

Survey of Recent Events (SRE)____
____
____

Life Experiences Survey (LES)____
____
____

Ways of Coping Scale____
____
____

Social Support____
____
____

Social Support Questionnaire (SSQ)___________________________________
____
____

Fill-in Questions

1. The Life Experiences Survey (LES) yields two separate scores for _______________ events, and one for _____________ events, making this instrument different from other life change measures.

2. The Ways of Coping Scale includes seven subscales that can be divided into _______________ or _______________ _______________ strategies for dealing with stressful situations.

Multiple-Choice Questions

1. One measure of life stress commonly used in psychiatric research is the
   a) SRE
   b) LCU
   c) AAT
   d) TAS
   e) any of the above could be used for this purpose

2. Which of the following constructs is <u>not</u> typically included in the definition of social support?
   a) financial assistance
   b) encouragement
   c) physical aid
   d) current life stress
   e) none of the above

Thought Question

1. Discuss the relationship between life stress and physical illness. (pages 445-447)

Answers

Terms, Concepts, and Names

Survey of Recent Events (SRE; p. 445)
Life Change Unit (LCU; pp. 445-446)
Life Experiences Survey (LES; p. 447)
Ways of Coping Scale (p. 448)
Social Support (p. 449)
Social Support Questionnaire (SSQ; p. 449)

Fill-in Questions

1. positive, negative (p. 447)
2. problem-focused, emotion-focused (p. 449)

Multiple-Choice Questions

1. a (p. 445)
2. d (p. 449)

Chapter 20

Testing in Health Care Settings

Terms, Concepts, and Names

Briefly identify the following:

Clinical neuropsychology ____________________

Learning Disability____________________

Halstead-Reitan Test Battery____________________

Luria-Nebraska Inventory____________________

pluripotentiality____________________

California Verbal Learning Test (CVLT)____________________

quality-of-life-assessment____________________

health status____________________

psychometric approach to quality-of-life-assessment____________________

decision theory approach to quality-of-life-assessment____________________

Sickness Impact Profile (SIP)____________________

Activities of Daily Living (ADL)____________________

Karnofsky Performance Status (KPS)______________________________
____
____

McMaster Health Index Questionnaire (MHIQ)________________________
____
____

Quality Adjusted Life Years (QALY)______________________________
____
____

Fill-in Questions

1. Clinical neuropsychology is a multi-disciplinary endeavor which overlaps with ____________________, ____________________, and ____________________.
2. ____________________ is an example of a learning disorder characterized by reading backwards.
3. The diversity of neuropsychological deficits identified by the ____________________ test could not be identified using more traditional psychometric tests.
4. One way to evaluate the health status of nations is in terms of their ____________________ ____________________ rates.
5. According to the WHO definition of health status, "health is a complete state of ____________________ , ____________________, and ____________________ well-being, and not merely the absence of disease."
6. The two major approaches to quality of life assessment are ____________________ and ____________________ ____________________.
7. The Sickness Impact Profile (SIP) is divided into three major clusters of items: ____________________ ____________________, ____________________, and ____________________.
8. The ____________________ is the most commonly used instrument to assess health in the elderly.
9. The Karnofsky Performance Status (KPS) has been used widely in ____________________ research.
10. The goal of the multi-disciplinary group of specialists who created the McMaster Health Index Questionnaire (MHIQ) was to develop an instrument that conforms with ____________________ ____________________.
11. Quality adjusted life years take into consideration the ____________________ consequences of various illnesses.

12. The approach to quality adjusted life years assessment described in this chapter classifies patients according to objective levels of functioning. These levels are represented by scales of ____________________, ____________________, and ____________________.

Multiple-Choice Questions

1. Most of the work in neuropsychology is directed toward the assessment of
   a) sensations/perceptions
   b) brain dysfunction
   c) mood
   d) motor movements
   e) learning

2. Which of the following neuropsychological tests emphasizes how errors are made in learning tasks?
   a) Luria-Nebraska
   b) Halstead-Reitan
   c) California Verbal Learning Test
   d) both a & c
   e) all of the above

3. An important characteristic that specifically identifies the Decision Theory Approach to quality of life assessment is that
   a) it provides separate measures for different dimensions of quality of life
   b) it asks respondents to choose from alternatives to determine what their quality of life is
   c) it is based upon subjective ratings by physicians
   d) it attempts to weight different dimensions of health
   e) all of the above

4. Scores on which of the following test(s) can be plotted on a graphic display similar to an MMPI profile?
   a) Sickness Impact Profile (SIP)
   b) Rand Health Insurance Measure
   c) McMaster Health Index Questionnaire (MHIQ)
   d) Index of Activities of Daily Living Scale (ADL)
   e) Karnofsky Performance Status (KPS)

5. A criticism of the Activities of Daily Living Scale (ADL) is that
   a) there is no documentation of validity
   b) it does not distinguish adequately between individuals who are at the well end of the quality of life continuum
   c) it is scored in too subjective a manner
   d) there are inadequate norms
   e) most persons obtain very low scores on the scale decreasing its utility for research

6. In cost/utility analysis, observable health states are weighted by
   a) utility judgments of quality
   b) an individual's level of productivity
   c) length of illness
   d) health care costs
   e) extent of treatment needed

Thought Questions

1. Discuss how an evaluation of quality of life contributes to our conceptualization of health status (pages 462-463).

2. Discuss some of the implications of the WHO's expanded definition of health (p. 462).

3. Describe the difficulty that is likely to be encountered when a researcher attempts to measure a relationship between variables with instruments that have low reliability. Note: it may be helpful to use a specific example (page 470).

Answers

Terms, Concepts, and Names

Clinical neuropsychology (p.453)
Learning Disability (p.454)
Halstead-Reitan (p.455)
Luria-Nebraska (p. 457)
pluripotentiality (p. 457)
California Verbal Learning Test (p. 460)
Quality of Life Assessment (pp. 461-462)
health status (p. 462)
psychometric approach (p. 463)
decision theory approach (p. 463)
Sickness Impact Profile (SIP; p. 464)
Activities of Daily Living (ADL; p. 464)
Karnofsky Performance Status (KPS; p. 468)
McMaster Health Index Questionnaire (MHIQ; p. 469)
quality adjusted life years (QALY; p. 470)

Fill-in Questions

1. Neurology, psychiatry, psychometric testing (p. 453)
2. Dyslexia (p. 454)
3. California Verbal Learning Test (CVLT; p. 460)
4. infant mortality (p. 462)
5. physical, mental, and social (p. 462)
6. psychometric, decision theory (p. 463)
7. Independent categories, physical, psychosocial (p. 464)
8. Activities of Daily Living (ADL; p. 464)
9. cancer (p. 468)

10. WHO definition of health (p. 469)
11. quality-of-life (p. 471)
12. mobility, physical activity, and social activity (pp. 471-472)

Multiple-Choice Questions

1. b (p. 453)
2. c (p. 460)
3. d (p. 463)
4. a (p. 464)
5. b (p. 466)
6. a (p. 470)

Chapter 21

Test Bias

Terms, Concepts, and Names

Briefly identify the following:

Uniform Guidelines on Employee Selection Procedures________________

differential validity________________

isodensity curve________________

the case of Larry P. v. Wilson Riles________________

Chitling Test________________

Black Intelligence Test of Cultural Homogeneity (BITCH) ________________

scientific racism________________

System of Multicultural Pluralistic Assessment (SOMPA)________________

Jane Mercer________________

estimated learning potentials (ELP's) ________________

Kaufman Assessment Battery for Children (K-ABC)________________

unqualified individualism____
____
____

straight regression system____
____
____

quota system ____
____
____

constant ratio system____
____
____

Cole/Darlington system____
____
____

differential process theory____
____
____

Fill-in Questions

1. The major purpose of the Chitling Test was to show that Blacks and Whites are just ______________________________.
2. The developers of the Black Intelligence Test of Cultural Homogeneity (BITCH) believed that for individuals in the black community it is more important to assess ____, than IQ.
3. The Black Intelligence Test of Cultural Homogeneity (BITCH) is most lacking psychometrically with regard to its __________.
4. The assumption underlying the System of Multicultural Pluralistic Assessment (SOMPA) is that cultural groups have the same ___________________________.
5. The only component of the System of Multicultural Pluralistic Assessment (SOMPA) that is typically adopted by traditional test users and developers is the ____________________.
6. Estimated learning potentials (ELP'S) are WISC-R scores that are adjusted for _____________________.
7. According to the ____________________ approach a test is fair if it finds the best candidates for a job or for admission to school.
8. The ___________________ approach represents the unqualified individualism position and has been favored by business because it assures the highest rate of productivity among selected employees.

9. Testing experts generally agree that intelligence and aptitude tests are valid for predictive purposes, however, their major concerns involve the interpretation and application of test results by ______________ ______________________________.

10. An example of the problem of finding appropriate criterion measures is seen with the Medical College Admission Test (MCAT). The MCAT predicts ________________________ but does not predict ____.

Multiple-Choice Questions

1. The main type of validity evidence that exists for the Chitling Test is
   a) predictive validity
   b) concurrent validity
   c) face validity
   d) content validity
   e) construct validity

2. The assessment technique which best challenges traditional beliefs about testing is the
   a) Black Intelligence Test of Cultural Homogeneity (BITCH)
   b) Chitling Test
   c) Dove Counterbalance General Intelligence Test
   d) System of Multicultural Pluralistic Assessment (SOMPA)
   e) none of the above

3. The System of Multicultural Pluralistic Assessment (SOMPA) attempts to integrate which three approaches to assessment?
   a) personal, social, and organizational
   b) personal, social, and medical
   c) individual, social, and pluralistic
   d) medical, social, and pluralistic
   e) medical, communal, and intellectual

4. Which System of Multicultural Pluralistic Assessment (SOMPA) model uses the norms **within** a particular group for defining deviance?
   a) pluralistic
   b) social
   c) organizational
   d) communal
   e) medical

5. Which of the following systems recognizes race and sex differences in selection decisions?
   a) unqualified individualism
   b) qualified individualism
   c) the quota system
   d) both a and b
   e) both b and c

Thought Questions

1. Two types of validity (content and criterion) are described in relation to test bias on pages 482-487 of your text. Both approaches to defining the meaning of a test suggest that certain tests (e.g., the SAT) are in fact **not** biased or, in other words, are not differentially valid. Discuss the findings that are presented and include your reasons for agreeing or disagreeing with them.

2. The originator of the System of Multicultural Pluralistic Assessment (SOMPA), Jane Mercer, has argued that it is important to label as many children as possible "normal" and to remove such children from EMR

classes. Her critics do not view labeling as such a damaging phenomenon and argue that these children will need special help anyway. Describe, in your opinion, what the advantages and disadvantages of the SOMPA approach are with regard to assessment and consequent placement decisions. (pages 494-496)

3. Which model of test fairness do you prefer and why? (pages 498-501)

Answers

Terms, Concepts, and Names

Uniform Guidelines on Employee Selection Procedures (p.481)
differential validity (p.482)
isodensity curve (p.486)
the case of Larry P. v. Wilson Riles (p.491)
Chitling Test (p.491)
Black Intelligence Test of Cultural Homogeneity (BITCH) (p. 493)
scientific racism (p.493)
System of Multicultural Pluralistic Assessment (SOMPA) (p.494)
Jane Mercer (p.494)
estimated learning potentials (ELP's) (p.496)
Kaufman Assessment Battery for Children (K-ABC) (p.497)
unqualified individualism (p.498)
straight regression system (p.499)
quota system (p.499)
constant ratio system (p.500)
Cole/Darlington system (p.500)
differential process theory (p.501)

Fill-in Questions

1. not talking the same language (p.492)
2. survival potential in the black community (p.493)
3. validity (p.493)
4. average potential (p.495)
5. social system portion (p.496)
6. socioeconomic background (p.496)
7. unqualified individualism (p.498)
8. straight regression (p.499)
9. elementary and secondary schools (p.501)
10. success in medical school, who will be a successful doctor (p.503)

Multiple-Choice Questions

1. c (p.492)
2. d (p.494)
3. d (p.495)
4. a (p.496)
5. e (p.499)

Chapter 22

Testing and the Law

Terms, Concepts, and Names

Briefly identify the following:

interstate commerce______________________________________

control of spending______________________________________

Equal Employment Opportunity Commission (EEOC) ________________

adverse impact____

four-fifths rule____

Truth in Testing Laws____________________________________

Education for All Handicapped Children Act of 1975________________

Plessy v. Ferguson______________________________________

Brown v. Board of Education________________________________

Stell v. Savannah-Chatham County Board of Education________________

Hobson v. Hansen_______________________________________

Diana v. State Board of Education______________________________

____

____

Larry P. v. Wilson Riles______________________________________

____

____

Parents in Action on Special Education v. Hannon__________________

____

____

Debra P. v. Turlington____

____

____

Regents of the University of California v. Bakke____________________

____

____

Golden Rule Insurance Company v. Washburn____________________

____

____

Connecticut v. Teal____

____

____

Fill-in Questions

1. The major intent of the Equal Employment Opportunity Commission (EEOC) guidelines is to ____________________.
2. The New York truth in testing law was motivated by an investigation of __________________________________.
3. The most controversial of the requirements set forth by the truth in testing law is that ____.
4. Pl (Public law) 94-142 guarantees a publicly financed education to ____.
5. The case of ______________________________ resulted in a set of special provisions for the testing of Mexican-American and Chinese-American children.
6. The effect of the ruling of the Larry P. v. Wilson Riles case was that ____.
   However, the ruling of Parents in Action on Special Education v. Hannon concluded that ____.
7. The Bakke decision involved a case of _________________________.

<u>Multiple-Choice Questions</u>

1. One of the most interesting problems with the four-fifths rule is that
   a) most employers find it uninterpretable
   b) efforts to recruit minority group members reduce the percentage from that group that is hired
   c) typically less than four-fifths of the applicants for a given job are minorities
   d) Numerous legal loopholes in the rule result in more discrimination than took place before its adoption
   e) all of the above

2. Which of the following cases resulted in the court ruling that schools must provide nonsegregated facilities for Black and White children?
   a) Brown v. Board of Education
   b) Plessy v. Ferguson
   c) Stell v. Savannah-Chatham County Board of Education
   d) Hobson v. Hansen
   e) Diana v. State Board of Education

3. A number of cases were attempts to resist the desegregation order. Many of these cases presented test scores which suggested that Black children were genetically incapable of learning in the same classroom as White children. One such case was
   a) Hobson v. Hansen
   b) Plessy v. Ferguson
   c) Brown v. Board of Education
   d) Stell v. Savannah-Chatham County Board of Education
   e) Diana V. State Board of Education

4. The type of test that came under scrutiny in the Debra P. v. Turlington case was a
   a) standard intelligence test
   b) multicultural pluralistic test
   c) personnel test
   d) minimum competency test
   e) graduate school selection test

Thought Questions

1. The controversial third portion of the Truth in Testing Law may cause serious problems for testing programs. Several of these problems are described in your text. Discuss these issues and include your views as to whether or not this section of the law should be retained. (pages 517-519)

2. In your opinion, what role should the courts play in the regulation of psychological tests and why?

Answers

Terms, Concepts, and Names

interstate commerce (p.509)
control of spending (p.510)
Equal Employment Opportunity Commission (EEOC) (p.510)
adverse impact (p.511)
four-fifths rule (p.511)
Truth in Testing Laws (p.517)
Education for All Handicapped Children Act of 1975 (p.520)
Plessy v. Ferguson (p.520)
Brown v. Board of Education (p.521)
Stell v. Savannah-Chatham County Board of Education (p.521)
Hobson v. Hansen (p.522)
Diana v. State Board of Education (p.523)
Larry P. v. Wilson Riles (p.524)

Parents in Action on Special Education v. Hannon (p.526)
Debra P. v. Turlington (p.530)
Regents of the University of California v. Bakke (p.532)
Golden Rule Insurance Company v. Washburn (p.533)
Connecticut v. Teal (p.535)

Fill-in Questions

1. prohibit discrimination (p.4510
2. the Educational Testing Service (ETS) (p.517)
3. on request by a student, a copy of the test questions, correct answers, and a student's answers must be provided (p.518)
4. all handicapped children (p.520)
5. Diana v. State Board of Education (p.523)
6. IQ tests could no longer be used to place Black children in EMR classes, evidence of racial bias in standardized IQ tests was not sufficient to disallow their use with Black children (pp. 524-526)
7. reverse discrimination (p.533)

Multiple-Choice Questions

1. b (p.511)
2. a (p.521)
3. d (p.521)
4. d (p.530)

Chapter 23

The Future of Psychological Testing

Terms, Concepts, and Names

Briefly identify the following:

theoretical concerns____

adequacy of tests____

actuarial prediction____

clinical prediction____

human rights____

labeling____

invasion of privacy____

confidentiality____

divided loyalties____

dehumanization____

usefulness of tests____
____
____

Fill-in Questions

1. One of the most important issues underlying tests is the ___________ of test results.
2. Most existing tests are presumed to measure a(n)__________.
3. An approach to analyzing test results which involves the use of a set of rules is called a(n)______________.
4. According to Dahlstrom (1969b), a person's privacy is only invaded when information obtained via psychological tests is used in ___________ ______________________________.
5. In order to resolve the conflict of divided loyalties a psychologist must ______________________________.
6. The public's general attitude toward psychological testing was described in your text as __________.
7. In the future it is likely that any test posing a real challenge to the Stanford-Binet and Wechsler tests will be based on ______________ and a more comprehensive theoretical rationale.
8. In contrast to earlier predictions, the ______________ is destined to be the premiere structured personality test of the twenty-first century.

Multiple-Choice Questions

1. While many individual and group tests have generally adequate reliability, just about any test could benefit from
   a) better validity documentation
   b) a larger standardization sample
   c) more representative norms
   d) simplified scoring techniques
   e) more standardized interpretations

2. Which of the following is a potential abuse inherent in the use of computer software to interpret psychological tests?
   a) use of software inappropriate to the client
   b) trivialization of assessment
   c) inadequate contribution of the clinician to the assessment process
   d) questionable computer-based interpretations
   e) all of the above

3. Current standards for test use state that the test constructor(s) must provide sufficient information to permit appropriate use of the test. Which of the following does **not** have to be included in this information?
   a) guidelines for administration and scoring
   b) information regarding item construction
   c) validity data
   d) reliability data
   e) description of the normative sample

4. The crucial social issue in testing is not whether tests are perfect but whether
   a) they are predictive of future behavior
   b) they are useful to society
   c) they can be used to make selection decisions
   d) they can measure current functioning adequately
   e) they can accurately measure skills and abilities

5. Which of the following is **not** related to the increased standards of test construction?
   a) a specific published set of standards for tests
   b) improved computer technology being used in the testing field
   c) increased objectivity in test construction
   d) administration of tests to a narrower, more specific range of individuals
   e) a continuing research interest in testing

Thought Questions

1. One of the theoretical issues underlying the use of psychological tests involves the stability of human characteristics. Using the information presented on pages 539-540 of your text as a framework discuss your views on this topic.

2. Discuss some of the negative consequences of "labeling" as presented on page 543 of your text. What might be some positive aspects of labeling? Discuss these as well.

Answers

Terms, Concepts, and Names

theoretical concerns (p.539)
adequacy of tests (p.541)
actuarial prediction (p.542)
clinical prediction (p.542)
human rights (p.543)
labeling (p.543)
invasion of privacy (p.544)
confidentiality (p.544)
divided loyalties (p.545)
dehumanization (p. 547)
usefulness of tests (p.547)

Fill-in Questions

1. dependability (reliability) (p.539)
2. stable entity (p.539)
3. actuarial approach (p.542)
4. inappropriate ways (p.544)
5. inform all concerned as to where his/her loyalty lies (p.545)
6. ambivalent (p.552)
7. original concepts (p.554)
8. MMPI (p.555)

Multiple-Choice Questions

1. a (p.541)
2. e (p.542)
3. b (p.546)
4. b (p.547)
5. d (pp.550-551)